UNDERSTANDING
— THE —
WINDSOR
REPORT

UNDERSTANDING
— THE —
WINDSOR
REPORT

Two Leaders in the American Church
Speak Across the Divide

IAN T. DOUGLAS
AND
PAUL F. M. ZAHL

*With a Comprehensive Report Summary
by Jan Nunley*

CHURCH PUBLISHING
New York

A catalog record for this book is available from the Library of Congress
ISBN 0-89869-487-6

Church Publishing Incorporated
445 Fifth Avenue
New York, NY 10016
www.churchpublishing.org

5 4 3 2 1

CONTENTS

A SUMMARY OF THE REPORT
AND ITS CONTEXT
Jan Nunley

A Note from the Publisher

When the full report of the Lambeth Commission on Communion, known more generally as the Windsor Report, was released to the public, it became clear to us at Church Publishing Inc. that the most useful service we could perform as an official publisher for the Episcopal Church would be to assist the faithful in understanding the meaning and implications of it. We invited two church leaders, with differing perspectives on the report and the events that occasioned it, to participate in a conversation about the report in light of historical, biblical, theological, ecclesiological, cultural, liturgical, and political issues. The conversation was conducted via email and edited for sense and flow by a member of our staff. The final "dialogue" was approved by Ian Douglas and Paul Zahl.

Because the Windsor Report itself is available to all on the Internet, we did not see the necessity of publishing it in book form. But we did sense the need for a comprehensive overview of the report's content and context so that readers of the Douglas-Zahl conversation would know the background for it. We also felt that such a summary would be a service to the church — and indeed, or perhaps especially, to those who are not part of the Anglican Communion. We asked Jan Nunley of Episcopal News Service to prepare this overview. At the end, she has added a summary of responses to the report that helps to frame the ongoing controversy in the church.

This book is as up-to-date as possible, concluding with events in March 2005. Our hope is that parishes will use it as an education tool, as a facilitator of dialogue among their members, and as a record of this important time in the life of the church. Individuals will also find much of interest here: *Understanding the Windsor Report* is a good read!

A DIALOGUE ON THE REPORT

Ian T. Douglas and Paul F. M. Zahl

AN INTRODUCTION
TO THE DISCUSSION
Ian T. Douglas

Individuals and groups in the Episcopal Church and the Anglican Communion who have an investment in the current conflicts over human sexuality (on both sides of the debate) might wonder how it is that two individuals who seem to have decidedly different perspectives on this hot-button issue can cooperate on a book in these difficult times. In particular, how can the dean of one of the most "conservative" Episcopalian seminaries, namely, Paul Zahl of Trinity Episcopal School for Ministry, sit down with a professor from one of the most "liberal" seminaries of the Episcopal Church, Ian Douglas of Episcopal Divinity School? Is there something in such a conversation that might point toward possibilities for reconciliation in the Anglican Communion in these turbulent times? Paul and I pray that it is so.

A word of introduction as to how this unlikely collaboration between Paul and myself came about and how we arrived at the conversational format for this book might be useful for the reader. In September 2004 I attended a Clergy Day for the Diocese of Massachusetts. In our sharing time with Bishop M. Thomas Shaw, SSJE, many questions were raised by the clericus as to what the Lambeth Commission on Communion might say in its report to be released in the following month and what authority the Commission's findings might have. Bishop Shaw did a masterful job answering many hard questions, but still anxiety and quandaries remained. At the end of the session, Bishop Shaw suggested that given my field of study, Mission and World Christianity, I might write a brief piece to help my clergy colleagues explain the work of the Lambeth Commission to their congregations. I, of course, responded, "Yes, Bishop."

At the same time many journalists with whom I have spoken over the years began to call me as they anticipated the release of the report of the Lambeth Commission. Many of the questions they asked were not dissimilar from those posed by the clergy of the Diocese of Massachusetts on Clergy Day. Taking into consideration both sets of questions, I quickly wrote "An Imagined Conversation on the Lambeth Commission." (The conversation may be found on the Web site of the Episcopal Divinity School under "resources" at *www.eds.edu.*) In "An Imagined Conversation" I tried to answer as many questions as possible for both church leaders and journalists with respect to where the Lambeth Commission came from and what it was that they were about to and/or might do. The response to "An Imagined Conversation" was quite positive, and many across the Episcopal Church and Anglican Communion, as well as in the media, found the document to be quite helpful and commented that the conversational format was both accessible and engaging. It seemed as if I was onto something here.

Shortly after "An Imagined Conversation" was made available and just as the "Windsor Report" was released by the Lambeth Commission, the Rev. Kenneth Arnold, publisher for Church Publishing Incorporated, approached me about writing a brief and quick book to help the Church "understand" what the Windsor Report is all about. Recalling the positive response to the conversational format of "An Imagined Conversation," I suggested to Ken that perhaps a lively and exciting way to engage the Windsor Report would be if I had a real conversation with someone who might see the Windsor Report, or at least the presenting circumstances for the work of the Lambeth Commission, very differently than I. Ken immediately warmed to the idea and asked who such a conversation partner might be.

For almost a decade I have had very warm and engaging interchanges with the Very Rev. Paul Zahl. We first met when we served together on the Steering Committee for the Episcopal

Church Foundation Fellows Forum. Both Paul and I are Episcopal Church Foundation Fellows, and we are now colleagues in the Episcopal seminary community. While Paul and I have not in the past, and do not currently, see eye to eye on many things in the church, there is a level of deep Christian respect, and yes, even brotherhood, that holds us together in our differences. Over the years Paul and I had toyed with the idea of a joint writing project as a witness to our commonality in Christ. Given that both Paul and I are very well versed in the contemporary goings-on of the Anglican Communion (he serves on the Inter-Anglican Theological and Doctrinal Commission and I on the Inter-Anglican Standing Commission on Mission and Evangelism as well as the Design Group for the 2008 Lambeth Conference), it immediately occurred to me that Paul might be the perfect conversation partner "across the divide" with whom to write the Windsor Report book. Ken liked the idea, and when approached Paul immediately said yes to the project. For Paul's openness and agreement to collaborate on this book, I will always be grateful.

The format that Paul and I arrived at for this book was pretty straightforward. Together we agreed on approximately twenty "starter" questions, which I initially drafted, roughly organized around the four sections of the Windsor Report. Paul and I then wrote our answers to the twenty or so questions and exchanged them by email. I must admit here that Paul was much more diligent and expeditious in writing his answers than I was. With each other's initial answers in hand we then wrote responses to what the other had initially drafted and then exchanged these responses, also by email. Thus for each of the approximately twenty original questions, Paul and I had a give-and-take of at least four exchanges. All of these questions, answers, and responses were shared along the way with our editor at Church Publishing Incorporated, Lucas Smith. It was Lucas who took our ramblings and musings and edited them into the coherent conversation that is now the substance of this book. We are deeply indebted to Lucas for his fine editing skills, and we also wish to extend our thanks to the publisher at Church Publishing, the Rev. Kenneth Arnold, for the invitation to do this book. The Episcopal Church and Anglican Communion are well served by these faithful ministers at Church Publishing.

Paul and I would like to thank our colleagues of the Episcopal Church Foundation Fellows Forum, for that is where so much of the genuine open-mindedness and common-mindedness that helped set the stage for our book originated. We would like to dedicate this book to our Anglican sisters and brothers around the world who have taught us much through the years about the gift of communion and what it means to be part of the world-wide Body of Christ. In particular we want to thank our friends and colleagues with whom we have served on the Inter-Anglican Theological and Doctrinal Commission, the Inter-Anglican Standing Commission on Mission and Evangelism, the Design Group for the 2008 Lambeth Conference, as well as those on the staff at the Anglican Communion Office and Lambeth Palace in London.

Finally, Paul and I believe that the fact that we have participated in this conversation across difference, and the lessons we have learned from each other in pursuing such, says as much about the nature of communion in Anglicanism, if not more so, than the words we have written. We offer our conversation across the divide to the Episcopal Church and the wider Anglican Communion in the firm belief that what unites us in Jesus Christ is always greater than that which divides us. For this, and for each other, we give thanks to God.

Chapter 1

How Did We Get Here?

Where did the Windsor Report come from?

IAN DOUGLAS: I think it is worthwhile to simply review, as straightforwardly as possible, where the Windsor Report came from. I am a student of institutional history, and I think we in the church often forget our ecclesial history at peril.

The Lambeth Commission on Communion, which drafted the Windsor Report, was a direct result of an "extraordinary meeting" of the primates of the Anglican Communion at Lambeth Palace on October 15–16, 2003. But questions related to the nature of communion in Anglicanism were also raised at the Lambeth Conference of 1998. As you know, Paul, the primates are the heads of the thirty-eight churches in the Anglican Communion, sometimes known as Archbishops, Presiding Bishops, Moderators, or Metropolitans. Great differences exist, however, across the Anglican Communion as to the role, authority, and power of these primates in each of their own churches. In the Episcopal Church we have an elected Presiding Bishop, the Rt. Rev. (or Most Rev.) Frank Griswold, who presides over the House of Bishops (thus the title Presiding Bishop). The primates were called to Lambeth Palace immediately after the decision of the August 2003 General Convention of the Episcopal Church giving consent to Bishop Robinson as Bishop of New Hampshire. This extraordinary meeting was called by Archbishop Williams so that the heads of the churches in the Anglican Communion could discuss the fact that for the first time an openly gay man living in a committed relationship with another man was to become a bishop in Anglicanism.

Thus the presenting issue that resulted in the calling of the extraordinary meeting of the primates of the Anglican Communion on October 15–16, 2003, by the Archbishop of Canterbury, Dr. Rowan Williams, was the consent given to the election of the Rt. Rev. V. Gene Robinson as Bishop of New Hampshire. This is undeniable, for the call to the heads of the churches of the Anglican Communion to come to Lambeth Palace, the residence and office of the Archbishop of Canterbury in London, was issued almost immediately after the General Convention decision in August 2003. I find it interesting, however, that such a call went immediately to the primates only and did not include other possible "consultative bodies" in Anglicanism, such as the Anglican Consultative Council or even the Inter-Anglican Theological and Doctrinal Commission, to say nothing of the Inter-Anglican Standing Commission on Mission and Evangelism. I do appreciate the significant and important role that the heads of the Anglican and United Churches play in the Anglican Communion, but are they the only body that needs to take council in difficult times?

PAUL ZAHL: In my view, the Windsor Report came as the result of a huge international protest on the part of traditional or conservative Anglican Christians against the election and consecration of an actively homosexual bishop, Gene Robinson, in the American diocese of New Hampshire.

So insistent and feeling was this outcry that the primates of the Anglican Communion called for an international commission to decide some agreed-upon response and course of action in relation to the protest.

The Windsor Report was necessary because an earlier task force, called the Inter-Anglican Theology and Doctrine Commission, had failed to anticipate the move in New Hampshire and was overwhelmed by the events of August 2003, when the gay bishop was approved by the Episcopal Church. It is extremely unlike Anglicanism, as it normally works (or doesn't), to move swiftly as well as decisively to determine anything. Yet the Eames Commission, which produced this Windsor Report, *had* to move.

The sharp forces, indeed the threats, affecting the international church were just so strong and so hot that something had to be done.

Speaking personally, I am disappointed with the outcome. But looking at it historically, it is almost a miracle that anything concrete came out at all. But it did.

ID: As to the product, I am both encouraged and concerned by the Windsor Report. There are some important offerings in the report that I think the Communion must take to heart. I am particularly thankful for the authority it gives to Scripture, the biblical hermeneutics it advances, and the underlying emphasis on relationships as basic to a life in communion. I am concerned, however, with the presentation, once again, of an instrumentalist approach to the maintenance of communion. I am not convinced that a reification of the Instruments of Unity (The Archbishop of Canterbury, The Lambeth Conference of Bishops, The Anglican Consultative Council, and the Primates Meeting) offers a life-giving approach to what it means to be an Anglican in today's world. I would much rather have seen a liturgical and missiological response rather than a structuralist/instrumentalist trajectory to the report. The fact that this did not happen is not a huge surprise to me, since the Commission included significant numbers of bishops, archbishops, and canon lawyers, and few if any missiologists (scholars of Christian mission). I know this sounds like sour grapes, but I do believe that the way forward for the Communion will not be found in canonical quick fixes or a clarification of church structures but rather in our common action in God's saving mission in the world.

PZ: Interestingly enough, to me, at least, I agree with you about the "institutional/hierarchical" tack of the Windsor Report. You are absolutely right that it amounts to a reification of the "instruments of unity" and is therefore a formal rather than a material response to the crisis. The report is thus completely *not* missiological.

What you spark in my mind is the initial objection I felt to the proposal entitled "To Mend the Net," which was submitted at Kanuga when the Inter-Anglican Theological and Doctrinal Commission was brought into being in a fresh incarnation. "To Mend the Net" had elements of prelacy implicit within it, rather than a full-bore exploration of the issues in theological terms themselves. In other words, the idea of some sort of structural discipline could be a wax nose to enforce uniformity from any side of an issue. Personally, I was in almost complete agreement, theologically and ethically, with the proposers of "To Mend the Net." But the means proposed to get us back on point felt a little Laudian potentially.

ID: While I assume that we are on different sides of the page with respect to the hot-button issue of the place of gay men and lesbians in the church, it appears as if we are reading the same text with respect to the structuralist/instrumentalists' responses proposed, be they the Windsor Report or "To Mend the Net." What amazes me is that folk across the Anglican Communion are so caught up in the issue that they often overlook the deeper ecclesiological issues afoot. Let me say that I am personally delighted, and not entirely surprised, that you and I share the same concerns about the Windsor Report with respect to the underlying ecclesiological positions espoused. The canonization of the "Four Instruments of Unity" beginning with the Virginia Report is of great concern to me. For although the Four Instruments can be seen as an exercise of conciliarity, they are far too episcopal and male for my like. Out of the eight hundred or so folk represented in the Four Instruments, fewer than forty are laypeople and fewer than forty are women. To build an ecclesiology of conciliarity around so many male bishops and archbishops is a real problem, I believe.

PZ: I am particularly concerned that attempts to manage structural or formal conformity or discipline not undermine the authentically pentecostal or "Holy Spirit" dimension of the church's life. Bishops, and instruments of unity, can err. They have and they can and they do. So I share your anxiety, if that is the right word, concerning the mechanism of the Windsor proposals. They involve that worrisome "reification" or objectification of which Rudolf Bultmann — not everybody's hero, I know — warned us so potently in the 1950s.

What is the nature and shape of the Anglican Communion today, and how did we get to this place?

PZ: The nature and shape of the Anglican Communion today is diffuse. The proper word is "dispersed." We do not possess a central or highly focused structure of authority. Our "bonds of affection" are either a fairly sentimental form of Anglophilia or the more specific theological affinity that evangelical Anglicans in Canada might feel with evangelical Anglicans in Kenya; or catholic Anglicans in Zimbabwe might feel with catholic Anglicans in Wisconsin, USA. Therefore what is exactly "Anglican" in the common ground is hard to pin down. The link to England or "Britishness" is inadequate to withstand strong pressure on the ground. Thus all the cautions in the world from the Archbishop of Canterbury before the approval of Gene Robinson were insufficient to deter ECUSA from its actions. And the real or steel links after the action proved to be theological or ideological in substance rather than sentimental. "Liberals" in South Africa tended to side with ECUSA. Evangelicals in East Africa almost all sided with conservatives in the USA. Anglican unities today tend to be unities of faith and morals rather than loyalty to the church as such. That, at least, has proven true in the aftermath of August 5, 2003.

I tend to see the nature and shape of the Communion as a wax nose. You can push it, like putty, into almost any shape you wish. Some people's Anglicanism, mine for example, is Protestant and evangelical. Others', however, is Catholic and modernist. And others' would be liberal and "broad church." In other words, I am reluctant to objectify Anglicanism as a distinct expression *in itself* of Christianity. Yes, there are certain broad Anglican distinctives, such as a high view of the importance of vertical inherited worship, a relatively "liberal" or tolerant take on what is unimportant or secondary (i.e., the so-called "adiaphora"), and a vision of church government that values unity in the form of a teaching proclaiming leader, the bishop. But these distinctives are not all that high contrast. They pale in comparison to the religious distinctives of Christianity such as Atonement, Trinity, Salvation, and the Holy Spirit. And when the hurricane of the surrounding world's culture makes landfall on the church, as it did in the historic instance of Gene Robinson, "bonds of affection" rooted in sentiment and historic memory alone snap!

ID: I know that you believe that the crisis in the Anglican Communion is all about sexuality, or more particularly homosexuality. I will not deny that recent actions by some churches in the Anglican Communion (in particular the Episcopal Church and the Anglican Church of Canada) to embrace gay and lesbian Christians in the life of the church in new ways have caused a great deal of concern and consternation across the Anglican Communion. I am not so naïve as to say that the fights going on within the Anglican Communion are not linked directly to human sexuality. As important as human sexuality is, and I believe that how a person comports him/herself in a physical relationship with another person has everything to do with matters of faithfulness and salvation, I believe that in the end the difficulties in today's Anglican Communion are not so much about sexuality as they are about power, authority, and identity. Please let me explain where I am coming from in this somewhat radical assertion.

As a student of Christian mission and world Christianity, with a decided methodological bias toward power analysis, I see the last half of the twentieth century (the period in which you and I have lived the majority of our lives) as one of the most exciting and wonderful periods in the history of Christianity. Mission scholars such as Andrew Walls of the University of Edinburgh and Lamin Sanneh of Yale have described this period as the advent of the Third Church, the Church of the Global South. During our lifetimes, Christianity has gone from being primarily identified with the Western Enlightenment world to a truly worldwide phenomenon. Never before in the history of the church has the gospel been proclaimed and lived in such a diversity of cultures, tongues, and peoples. We are truly in the midst of a New Pentecost. Thanks be to God.

Now the church into which we were born (and I'm speaking specifically of Anglicanism here) was primarily identified with an English-speaking, North Atlantic alliance of England and the United States. That is no longer the case. Today, the Anglican Communion, this family of churches of which the Episcopal Church is but one entity, is made up of thirty-eight regional or national churches, located in 164 countries with upwards of 75 million members. Most of this growth in Anglicanism around the world has occurred in places and cultures very different from England and the United States, in areas of the world that would have been our colonies in the bad old days of imperialism. So a fundamental reality of Anglicanism in our lifetime is that we have moved from a monocultural English-identified church to a radically multicultural church made up of a vast plurality of cultures, peoples, and languages. This change from a monocultural, dare I say hegemonic, Anglo-American church to a multicultural family of churches has called into question often unexamined assumptions of who is an Anglican and what it means to be an Anglican today, to say nothing of who gets to decide.

Now if the changes in world Christianity were not enough to shake the foundations of what it means to be an Anglican Christian today, the changes closer to home in the Episcopal Church have been equally radical. During our lifetime, the Episcopal Church has begun to hear the voices of people and communities that historically have been more marginal, more excluded from the power structures of the church. Recall when Mohammed Kenyatta and the Rev. Paul Washington seized the microphone from Presiding Bishop John Hines at a plenary session of the Special General Convention of 1969, challenging the Episcopal Church to respond to the civil rights movement in the United States. The inclusion of women as Deputies to the General Convention in 1970 and the ordination of women, "irregularly" in 1974 and then officially beginning in 1976, challenged the supremacy of men in the councils and ordained leadership of the church. The "new" Prayer Book of 1979, and the primacy it gives to baptism and the "priesthood of all believers," has begun to undercut the rampant clericalism in the church. And now initial steps of gay and lesbian Christians to claim a full place in the life of the church are beginning to occur. (Would that the Episcopal Church was moving as quickly on issues of classism and elitism.)

I believe that these changes in Anglicanism globally, and in the Episcopal Church more locally, are profoundly upsetting for those of us who have been the most privileged, most secure, in our Anglo-American hegemony (namely, people like you and me, Paul, namely, primarily English-speaking, white, male, heterosexual, overly educated, financially secure, U.S. passport–holding, American clergy). Our historic unchallenged power to decide what is right, who is in and who is out, is now coming under attack. I believe that is a good thing, because if salvation was limited to those who look and act only like you and me (even given our theological differences), heaven would sure be a lonely place.

PZ: Ian, I want to take you on here just a little. While I agree with you about power — for it is an eviscerating factor in church life, in Christian life, in all life — is the fuss really reducible to that? Maybe "psychologically" or emotionally, it is. And yes, the American hegemony really does need challenging. You are doing that. I say, Right On! (Which is thoroughly Sixties slang!) But I still think we do the idea of truth a disservice if we do not deal with the question itself on its own terms. That is not to prejudge the question, by the way. But it is to take it most seriously, and at face value.

Like Cat Stevens, who is now a militant Muslim, "I'm looking for a moon shadow" — which is to say, I am looking for a "liberal" Episcopalian who is actually willing to talk at depth and length with me about the substantive objection that St. Paul raises to homosexuality qua homosexuality in the first part of Romans. How can we really say that St. Paul doesn't mean what he says?

Just raising the point, because power is deconstructible, but I fear it is not the only "discussable" here.

ID: Fair enough, Paul. It is crucially important that the Anglican Communion have some genuine and deep theological discussion about the place of gay and lesbian Christians in the life of the church today. And we do need to wrestle with such scripturally, in a reasoned manner, and taking the tradition seriously. I think that Lambeth 1998 Resolution 1:10 asked for such when it called us to listen to the experience of homosexual persons in the church. The problem is that all of us, on both sides of these questions, have been so busy lobbing polemical grenades back and forth that we have not stopped to listen genuinely to each side. The hurt that exists on both sides has caused us to be deaf to hearing from the other. That, to me, is a real tragedy.

But then again, I am not of the belief that single-identity politics gets us closer to the Reign of God in any way or manner. The human condition, the human gift, is that God has created us, individually and corporately, with so many complexities and points of identity, such as sexuality, gender, race, class, age, language, national origin, clerical status, etc., etc. Fighting over one aspect of identity at the exclusion of the fullness of who we are will necessarily result in a dualistic, either/or, "I'm right and you're wrong" fight that to me is a dead end for conversation and conversion.

What is the nature of the crisis in the Communion?

PZ: I see the crisis in the Communion as a crisis of faith and also as a crisis of selfishness. It is a crisis of faith because ECUSA's grasp of the Christian religion has proven to be an easy target for takeover by forces in the world such as the gay community's hunger for blessing from the church. ECUSA — and I have lived within it since I was a boy — has become too receptive, as I see it, or too undefended, in relation to whatever the world is saying at this particular point in our contemporaneity. The church's breakfronts against cultural takeovers have been too low. We have not been orthodox or clear enough to withstand the tides of the time. The

Episcopal Church was an easy target for any number of agendas imported from outside it. What I think the crisis in the Anglican Communion points to is the "soft" character of Anglicanism's mainstream expression in North America.

So there is a faith crisis, right up against our faces.

ID: I agree with you Paul, there is a crisis in the Anglican Communion. But that crisis is less, I believe, about the loss of theological orthodoxy per se (what you describe as a crisis of faith) than about the loss of the Church, and the Anglican Communion, as we have known it for the last two decades. Now I do understand that I can take this position because, unlike you, I do not see questions of human sexuality as striking at the very essence of the church. I do not subscribe to a conspiracy theory that posits there is some "cultural takeover" or "agenda imported from outside" that is seeking to destroy the church. Now maybe I misunderstand what you are saying, but I do not think there is any true gospel, or true church, that can be divorced from the cultural context in which the followers of Christ are located. The mystery of the Incarnation, for me, is that while God became fully human in the particularities of a first-century Jew in Palestine, the saving (yes, atoning) love of God in Jesus Christ became universally accessible for all people. The universal truth of God in Jesus Christ thus must always be known in the finiteness and particularities of specific cultural contexts. Our mutual friend Titus Presler likes to call this mystery of the Incarnation where universal truth can be known only in particularities of cultural contexts as the tension and embrace of gospel and culture. The gospel is always in tension with and embracing the culture in which it is located. The crisis before the Anglican Communion then is not so much about orthodoxy (right belief) but rather orthopraxis (right action). How do the radically different cultures of the Anglican Communion (not forgetting that in each cultural context the gospel is both in tension and embraced) come to share a common life, common practice, and common participation in the Good News of Jesus Christ?

PZ: But that is not all. It is also a crisis of selfishness. The American Church reflected the intrinsic narcissism of much of the American self-understanding in general. We do not care what the rest of the world thinks about what we do. We do not factor that in, not at all. When eleven million Europeans marched against the Iraq War, and even the Pope opposed it publicly, the American President referred to all that as a "focus group." The American Presiding Bishop has acted just like the American President! The Primates of the Communion asked him not to consecrate Gene Robinson — they *told* him not to do it in a most forceful manner. But he "did it just the same" ("Sex Crime" by Eurythmics). The rest of the world — I mean just about the whole rest of the world — called on George W. Bush to think again before going forward with the preemptive invasion of Iraq. But he "did it just the same."

The nature of our crisis is thus not just theological, for it involves a totally one-sided approach on the part of ECUSA to "process." On the other hand, the nature of the crisis is not solely American-style unilateralism. This is because there is a theological superficiality to ECUSA which the crisis has quite dramatically unmasked.

The crisis of the Communion is deep and also panoramic. About these two adjectives concerning the thing, I feel that we are agreed.

ID: Having disagreed with you on the nature of the faith crisis, I do agree with you in your description of the crisis of selfishness (particularly as it applies to the Episcopal Church and the United States in the world today). Here I would say that it is less a crisis of selfishness and more a crisis of unknowing. Now you will have to oblige me my use of power analysis again. The funny thing (or perhaps better said, the sinful thing) about how power works is that those who are most privileged, most in power, are blind to the power that they have. Sin being what it is, the powerful are able to define the world as if only their reality exists. Peggy Macintosh of Wellesley College, in considering matters of race in the United States, has described the "invisible knapsack" of white privilege. White people in the United States are able to believe that racism does not really exist because they do not experience its destructive forces. They have the power to say that there is really no difference between them and people of color, while the reality of people of color, who live with the insidiousness of racism every day in the United States, is radically different.

The same is true for the United States and for the Episcopal Church. Given our economic, military, political, and cultural power, the United States is able to believe that what we take as true and right is normative for the whole world. We perceive that our definitions of freedom, what is right and what is wrong, who is and is not a terrorist, and our embrace of liberal economics and the free market, is what all people believe to be true and hold dear the world over. Our power blinds us from the fact that many people, nations, and cultures around the world simply do not see the world as we do.

And it is the same for the Episcopal Church. Our economic, political, cultural, and yes, ecclesial, power has often blinded us from the fact that other churches exist. I remember that when I worked in the World Mission Department at the Episcopal Church Center in New York in the early 1980s I was continually amazed that Anglicans around the world always knew so much more about ECUSA than we did about the CPK (Church of the Province of Kenya), CPSA (Church of the Province of Southern Africa), or even the CPWI (Church of the Province of the West Indies). Knowing the master's tools was an element of survival for these folks. Even if we recognize today that there are indeed churches other than our own in the Anglican Communion (this is an interesting and beneficial result of the current crisis), many Episcopalians have a hard time believing that these sisters and brothers in Christ might not share our worldview on very key concerns and beliefs that we hold dear. Our lingering sins of racism and colonialism, coupled with our power and dominance in the world and the Anglican Communion, lets us dismiss sisters and brothers around the world as "superstitious" or "premodern," as one bishop was quoted as saying at Lambeth 1998.

The linking of our power in the United States with the ecclesial power of the Episcopal Church came home to me at one inter-Anglican meeting a few months after the General Convention of 2003. I attended a ten-day meeting with twenty-one other sisters and brothers in Christ from twenty-one other churches of the Anglican Communion. Being an American, I, of course, wanted to get right into the issues that seemed to divide us. It wasn't until the eighth day of the meeting, however, that we began to discuss the General Convention. The conversation was spirited, honest, loving, and difficult. Perhaps the biggest learning of the day for me was the fact that all twenty-one Anglicans from other parts of the world (even those who personally and as representatives of their churches supported the decisions of our General Convention) fundamentally agreed with what one sister in the meeting offered when she said: "Ian, please understand us. For us there is no difference between Gene Robinson and George Bush." Such is the reality of sisters and brothers in Christ who live in radically different, and less powerful, situations than we do.

PZ: We are agreed about the USA and the "American" aspect of ECUSA. I like your adjective "unknowing." We live within the "cloud of unknowing." I immediately thought of that gloriously kitschy sci-fi movie of 1959 entitled *The Crawling Eye*. It was made in England, by the way, by an English creative team. (Using the word "creative" liberally....) But in the movie there is a huge cloud encircling one of the Swiss Alps. Everyone who tries to climb up and pierce the cloud, and find out what is there, disappears and dies. It is a cloud that is impenetrable, an objectified cloud of unknowing.

Unfortunately, however, it is a little worse than that. For huge eye-creatures from another planet have taken up residence in the cloud. From within the cloud, they are planning an alien invasion of ... Earth.

That is the kind of art that gives one hope!

But seriously, while I do not believe in "conspiracy" theories vis-à-vis our church, I do want to say that you and I differ over the question of whether the consecration of an actively gay bishop is church-dividing. I believe it is church-dividing. It is church-dividing not because it imperils biblical authority, although it does. It is church-dividing because the backers of the idea have a different doctrine of the human being; an Arminian anthropology; a very different view of Original Sin (from, say, the Articles); a reduced view of substitutionary atonement; and thus, too, a lower Christology than is orthodox. I don't think they have an insufficient doctrine of the Trinity — nor perhaps even a defective view of the Incarnation. But the problems with their anthropology are extremely important.

So to me, while I may be able to agree with you that it might not be *definitely* church-dividing, I think the implications of the consecration probably are. But hey, "Let's [continue to] Talk" (Joan Rivers).

ID: Yup, you and I definitely are at different places here. I do not think the "consecration of an actively gay bishop" is necessarily church-dividing. Call me naïve, call me hopeful, call me stupid, but I simply refuse to believe that this is the end for the church or for that matter, the Anglican Communion. As long as we keep talking, and coming to the table as repentant sinners to be fed with the Body and Blood of Christ, then I think all things are possible. (I do hope we talk about the place of liturgy in the Anglican Communion as holding us together at some point.) So yes, let's keep talking.

How has the changing face of the Communion affected our understanding of "communion"?

PZ: By the changing face of the Communion is meant the fact of its being a face of color! In other words, nonwhite Anglicans now far outnumber white Anglicans. This means that evangelical or traditional Anglicans far outnumber liberal or Western Anglicans. The nineteenth-century missionaries from England did their work well. Organizations like the CMS (Church Missionary Society) brought the "Old, Old Story" of Christ to Africa and India and

Asia, and the descendants of their first converts now speak for the Anglican Church in most regions of the world.

It always used to make me smile (or maybe wince) when liberal American Episcopal bishops would return from Africa impressed with the faith and spirituality of their hosts only to sneer at evangelicals back home. They did not seem to realize that the Africans' piety was not an African thing, but a gospel thing. Our bishops were and often are still unable to see that the religious passion of the Two-Thirds-Worlders has come especially from an evangelical Christian West one hundred years ago, and has simply not changed. As Bishop Edward Salmon of South Carolina sometimes says, speaking as a conservative, "It's not we who have changed: it is ECUSA that has changed, and moved on, and made us appear to be ancient whales, beached upon the shore."

ID: I am pleased, Paul, that you and I both share an appreciation of what God is bringing into being in other parts of the world church. I rejoice in the fact that you and I have been fortunate to travel, experience, and come to know deeply the dynamism (and the difficulties) of Anglican churches around the world. I think I speak for both of us in saying that we have experienced a profound conversion, a turning around, of what we understand as the Body of Christ because of the time we have spent with Anglican sisters and brothers from other parts of the world.

I do not, however, share your perspective that Anglicanism in Africa, Asia, Latin America, and the Pacific (or in any one region thereof) is monochromatic, uniform, and solidly evangelical and traditional. I believe the presentation of "the South" as always being united in one perspective and of one voice is a construction of those, especially those in the West, who want to enlist some imagined unified authoritarian Southern voice in our battles over human sexuality in the West. And I might add here that leaders in Africa, Asia, Latin America, and the Pacific are often all too happy to paper over their own differences if it buys them a certain amount of cachet or voice on the global stage of church debates.

I also do not share your position (if I understand you correctly) that the "evangelical or traditional" commitments of Anglicans in the global South are a result primarily of good work of nineteenth-century missionaries from England who "brought the 'Old, Old Story' of Christ to Africa and India and Asia." True, the selfless efforts of missionaries from England, the United States, and other older sending churches of the West need to be celebrated as contributing to the new Pentecost of world Christianity today. But I am enough of a student of Lamin Sanneh to see that the growth of churches in Africa, Asia, Latin America, and the Pacific is more a result of indigenous agents, empowered by the Holy Spirit, who have worked tirelessly translating the gospel into the vernacular and cultural contexts of their own people.

PZ: The changing evangelical/conservative Christian face of the Anglican Communion has affected our understanding of "communion" because this new face values Scripture and truth, and personal holiness as the Windsor Report emphasizes, more than it does sentiment and history. Yes, they do often value the British link. They do appreciate the Commonwealth and the continuity of form and ceremony and historic heritage. But they will almost always wish to trump all that, the legacy part, with the greater inherited truth claims of the Bible. This comes through loud and clear whenever the African bishops speak, as, for example, in the CAPA statement of October 2004. They preach to us now. And it makes my heart glad.

What I am saying is that the conservative Christianity of the new face of Anglicanism threatens "communion" in the old formal sense. I myself feel that I hold almost limitlessly more in common with each Ugandan bishop than with well over half of the bishops of my own province, ECUSA. Thus "communion" for me means theological communion or common ground rather than romanticized "bonds of affection" with Canterbury, Lambeth, New York, and First-World Anglicanism in general. What a bizarre script! One finds oneself regarding many in one's own denomination as being "strangers in the night" rather than brothers and sisters in Christ. I truly wish this were not so. But the changing face of the Communion *has* affected my sense of who I am in and who I am not in any binding or heartfelt communion with.

ID: I guess I fundamentally do not agree with those who, like Philip Jenkins, argue that there is a unified "New Christendom" that is evangelical, conservative, and out to get a liberal errant West. Such defines what God is doing anew in Africa, Asia, Latin America, and the Pacific in terms of our definitions, our history: the history of Christendom rather than the story of a New Pentecost. New Christendom positions keep us in the West in the center of the conversation, and the truth of the matter is we no longer occupy such a position. Similarly I am not a fan of Samuel Huntington's "clash of civilizations" theory, for such advances a dualistic "West versus the West" mentality that denies the uniqueness and particularities of what God in Jesus Christ is doing in all of our different cultural contexts.

The emerging churches of the global South (in all their differences and pluralities) are not some uniform knockoff of an evangelical Victorian Church. God is indeed doing a new thing in them, and we need to appreciate that there is as much diversity and problems among the churches of the South as there has ever been, or is today, in the churches of the West.

So perhaps you can see that I am indeed excited about what God is up to in the emergence of World Christianity, and this has everything to do with why I am so passionate about the Anglican Communion at this particular time.

PZ: We both share the same encouragement from the "Global South." We both are strengthened, even given life from the dead, by our brothers and sisters below the Equator.

Our only difference on this question is a matter of the data. Is the "Global South" generally evangelical and/or Pentecostal, or not? And whence the seed of it? You have evidence that the South is not monochrome. You also see the present vitality of the Spirit in several sectors as being un-derived from the Victorian missionary movement. I am happy to grant you the second point, although the organic link still seems to me to be the nineteenth-century evangelists from Britain and North America.

But I am not convinced that Global South Anglicanism is not, numerically speaking at least, quite "orthodox" in the present sense of that word. Everywhere I have gone, it has looked, whether it be "catholic" or "protestant" in its Anglican expression, pretty "conservative" by Diocese of New York standards. I have always wondered why you don't agree with Philip Jenkins — at least concerning the empirical data.

But then again, maybe you and Titus know something I do not. I have to take your word for it.

ID: Your clause "by Diocese of New York standards" gives you away. I agree with you that if we use New York eyes, then the majority of the Anglican Communion looks pretty "conservative." The point I am trying to make is that we have to stop using New York, or Washington, or Pittsburgh, or Dallas, or London, or Oxford, or Cambridge eyes to "see" what God is up to in the Anglican Communion today. We simply have to stop using our frame of reference to see and understand what God is doing in the world today.

I remember when I was a missionary in Haiti in the early 1980s. Many Haitians would come up to me and ask if I was a missionary (which most white people in Haiti were at the time). In my good, white, liberal, Northeast guilt over what I thought missionaries had done in centuries past, I would not own the label of missionary. Rather I would describe myself as a church-worker who had come to work as a volunteer partner with the Episcopal Church of Haiti. After months of saying such, a kind and caring Haitian Christian brother said to me: "Why are you so worried about being called a missionary? If it is about the evils that missionaries have done in the past, I can understand your concern. But what you have to understand is that as long as you are primarily concerned about what the missionaries have done in the past or today, then the focus is still on you. I'm here to tell you the focus is no longer on you the missionary but on us, the Church, in Haiti. Please get over your self-centeredness and your concerns about self-definitions, and join with us in the work we have to do together." Now there was a real wake-up call for me! I had to realize that as long as I was attempting to define the terms, I was keeping myself in the center of the conversation.

The reality was, and is, that I am not in the center but rather at the margins of the Christian witness in the world today. This is tremendously humbling and at the same time tremendously liberating. Since that conversation in Haiti, I have had no problem seeing myself as a missionary.

And here is my real beef with Philip Jenkins. It is not that I disagree with his empirical demographic data. I do not. (Just a note, here: Jenkins's data all comes from good missiologists like David Barrett and Andrew Walls, for both of whom I have the greatest of respect and admiration.) What I disagree with Jenkins about is that he uses our definitions in the West to define and categorize what God is up to in the rest of the world today. Even his title "The Next Christendom" uses our historical record and construct to portray the New Pentecost in the Global South; to say nothing of the way that Jenkins uses the emergence of the Church in Africa, Asia, and Latin America as ammunition in the liberal/conservative infighting in the Church of the West. So it is not the data that I take exception to in Jenkins's book, but rather the way he uses our Western definitions and politics to interpret the data.

Why should anyone care about the Windsor Report, or the Anglican Communion for that matter?

ID: As catholic Christians, Christians who believe that God in Jesus Christ has bound us together with sisters and brothers in Christ across time and space, we cannot live in isolation unto ourselves. We cannot function as if we have no need for the other. For our salvation, the fullness of life in Christ necessitates that we live entwined with those who are radically different than we are. I believe that I cannot know the fullness of what God has done in Jesus Christ unless I am connected to others who are radically different than I am. I need folk who are very different from who I am in order to live into what God has done in and for the world in Jesus. Max Warren, the historic General Secretary of the English Church Missionary Society, said it best when he said, "It takes the whole world to know the whole Gospel."

So why should I care about the Windsor Report? I should care because it represents one understanding of how Anglicans are struggling to stay connected to each other, stay in communion with each other. And being in communion with each other means that I am brought into the fullness of God in Christ through being interdependently related to those who are so different than I am. Do I think it is the best way to stay in Communion? Far from it, and I hope we can discuss some of my misgivings about the report. But still the Windsor Report is the currency of conversation right now as to the nature of Communion for Anglicans today.

PZ: The Windsor Report is very important. For Christian believers, it is of intrinsic interest because it seeks to position some classic formal theology in close applied relation with our present problems. There is a pathos, for better or worse, to this fresh attempt to grapple theologically with a big agenda arising from the "present age." The Eames Commission has tried to do something.

But there is also a historic significance to the report. It flags, or is flagged by, the great new divide in world Christianity between the Two-Thirds World, with its assertive vital evangelicalism and Pentecostalism, and the First World, with our washed out "nuanced" convictions and permeable openness — meaning capitulation — to the spirit of the age. The Windsor Report embodies something, and it also symbolizes something. It embodies the great divide between southern hemisphere and northern hemisphere Christians. And it symbolizes a certain tragic inability to speak convincingly across that divide. Certainly this means I am skeptical about the positive "results" of the report. But I am also sympathetic to what it is seeking to do and also the seriousness of what it has failed to do.

The Windsor Report therefore carries interest for almost everyone, even for those interested only in its sociological or historical meaning. Because the American Episcopal Church was the first of the old orthodox and liturgical mainstream churches in the influential United States to prove itself utterly vulnerable to a cultural takeover from the "left," the relation of ECUSA to its world partners in Christianity became a flash point, *the* flash point, I would say, for the "culture wars" between Western versions of personal morality and the traditional versions of personal morality held by most people of color. The consecration of Gene Robinson catalyzed the great divide about which so many observers of world religion and culture are now writing.

The presenting problem addressed by the Windsor Report — which, despite all the explicit reluctance of the Commission to get remotely near it, is homosexuality in Christian perspective — touches on another, most timely question. This is the relation of the West to the religion of Islam. Conservative Christians in the West regard the culture of secular and sexual materialism that surrounds them with something of the same appalledness with which Muslims regard that culture. We sympathize, in other words, with the Islamic critique of Western lifestyles. This is tied up with the extremely defensive reaction of at least two of the Western democracies, i.e., the UK and the USA, to the September 11 attacks. We, in those two democracies, did not wish to know about what radical Islam was asserting and acting on. Anyone in the conservative Christian community who touched the question of ethical decadence in the West was instantly silenced, then sentenced to the living death of being a leper. Jerry Falwell fell into this terminal trap, with several others in the same school of thought. And then the link was made by the world between "Christian" fundamentalism and the reacting values of Islamic Jihad. The link has not been foresworn.

The brand of Christianity espoused by most Two-Thirds-World Christians is almost as critical of Western Christianity as Islam is. No wonder "liberal" Christians of ECUSA howl in outrage when they are criticized, even ostracized, by conservatives from the World South. It is Jerry Falwell and Pat Robertson all over again.

The Windsor Report is dealing in the currency of extreme cultural stress and widespread division. I am sometimes surprised that the world at large has not made more of it than it has.

Now, why ought someone be interested in the Anglican Communion in its own terms? The answer to this question is less obvious than the answer to the first. Is the Anglican Communion interesting in itself?

I tend to think not. A church that is, in its DNA, to use the current phrase, so dispersed, ambiguous, and ambivalent in its core assertions and theological goods is probably less worthy of general attention than the Southern Baptist Convention, for example, which seems to evince extreme countercultural primal force. There is always a segment of the religious community which values aesthetics. (It is a small segment.) In other words, there are people who value "Anglicanism" as a sort of special subset or genre of religious believing. But the things which are treasured in that "Anglicanism" are low-octane. They fall under the heading "Christianity lite," at least by comparison with Spanish-speaking Pentecostalism or East African revivalism.

It simply has to be said. The Anglican Communion as such is penultimate. I have lived in it and served from it for years and years. Ian, you have, too. There are therefore some important "bonds of affection" you and I both share, simply because we have each sought to give so much to it, and have lived so engagedly in it, for decades and decades. But does Anglicanism *as such* possess the emotional urgency to awaken you in the middle of the night? Does it have one-tenth of the urgency from which Marvin Gaye sang so successfully twenty years ago: "Wake up, wake up, wake up, wake up — let's dah-dah-dah-dah..."? I cannot imagine that it has.

So yes, Anglicanism, permeable to the world in its Western expression, is a flash point of division. It is like the Ardoyne Road area of North Belfast. In itself, the Road is unremarkable. But it became interesting when Sinn Fein hijacked its vulnerable location in order to drive the Protestant residents out. Thus the American Episcopal Church is a fairly low-energy phenomenon. But it got itself hijacked. And now, in the light of 9/11 and the awesome empirical divide through worldwide Christianity, its captivated case sums up an almost world historical problem.

ID: On the question of Islam, yes I would agree with you that we in the Anglican Communion have a very complex and difficult relationship to the followers of Muhammad. On one side there are those of us (particularly those of us who do not live under the threat of a militant aggressive and expanding Muslim presence) who want to have a dialogical, mutually beneficial exchange with the adherents of another stream of the Abrahamic faith. We seek understanding, mutual respect, and forbearance in a post-9/11 world where all too often the "terrorists" are uncritically presented as Muslim fundamentalists. Yet there are other Anglicans for whom "dialogue means death," as I have heard from some colleagues in the Communion. The difficult and often oppressive realities that Anglican sisters and brothers live with daily, where Christian believers are systematically killed and churches are burned by Islamic extremists, cannot be denied or left unheeded. I do agree that, given the interdependence and perceived unity of the Anglican Communion, decisions taken in the West (particularly with respect to the inclusion of gay and lesbian people in the life of the church) become yet another reason for the oppression of Anglicans living close to or under Islamic rule. We cannot deny the fact that we as Anglicans are profoundly related one to another and that decisions taken in one corner of the Communion do have important and lasting effects on other parts of the Communion. This is especially true for the more marginal and persecuted churches in the Communion.

PZ: I don't think you fully engaged on this one, although you have approached the question of Islam. We are both agreed that for historical reasons, our Anglican Church is at the flashpoint of post-9/11 anxieties because our fellow Christians in several areas of the world are in harsh vulnerability over against militant Islam.

You have also said that the Anglican Church is "interesting" because we are a part of the Church catholic and universal, and that is interesting in itself.

I was trying to state that Anglicanism as such is really not interesting. I mean, it is interesting a little, but its "low-octane" concerns in many corners make it less "core" or fundamental in its cosmetic fascination for the world. Where Anglicanism gets "interesting" is where it gets passionate about the deep questions of life. It is interesting when the ALPHA course gets going in massively secular and post-Christian London. It is interesting when the Rector of Drumcree Parish Church in Northern Ireland becomes a peace broker of astonishing countercultural force. It is interesting when the Bishop of Jos in Nigeria barely escapes with his life during anti-Christian riots by Muslims there.

But it is not particularly interesting when it concerns "Englishness" (which no longer exists, by the way), kneelers, and ecclesiasticism. I think we actually are side by side on this perspective.

ID: We sure are "side by side on this perspective." I could not agree with you more. Anglicanism (and any other Christian tradition for that matter) really only makes sense, has meaning, when it becomes the crucible in which the life-changing, reconciling, restoring mission of God is lived out in the real-life, incarnational realities of people's lives. So amen, brother.

Chapter 2

WHAT DOES THE BIBLE SAY?

What are the main biblical sources used in the Windsor Report? What "biblical foundations" are advanced?

IAN DOUGLAS: Paul, you are so much better a biblical scholar than I am that I go to this next section with fear and trembling. I respect your grasp of Scripture and your command of biblical languages so much that I wonder if I should just throw in the towel here. But since I see this conversation not as a fifteen-round heavyweight bout but rather an exercise of Christian brothers in a mutual search for truth and understanding, I am more than willing to go to the mat on the Bible with you.

PAUL ZAHL: Well, Ian, the main biblical sources used in the report are Ephesians and 1 Corinthians. Ephesians is mustered in to lend a lofty opening description of "church," and to invoke the character of church as an eschatological sign of the eventually-to-be-fulfilled Kingdom of God. This is the "high church" section of the report (sec. A.2) and makes me uncomfortable. Such claims concerning "redeemed unity" and the like tend to make me want to reach for my holster. I fear that celestial claims predicated to "church" are able to bolster exaggerated and arbitrary church-manship. And in the light of our present divisions and dissensions, we need, I feel, to *lower* our aspirations on behalf of the visible church, not magnify them.

ID: Your description of Ephesians and 1 Corinthians as the basic biblical sources in the report is correct. I somewhat agree with you that "Ephesians is mustered in to lend a lofty opening description of 'church.'" I am more sympathetic to this perspective than you seem to be. Perhaps I am more "high church" in my piety that you are, but I do not have much difficulty with seeing the church (and I mean here not the institution but the Body of Christ) as an "*anticipatory sign* of God's healing and restorative future for the world" (par. 2). I do believe that the Body of Christ has been called, and uniquely empowered, to be an agent of God's reconciling, restoring, and restorative action in the world. So Ephesians, right on.

PZ: The other main source for the first salvo of the report is the "body" and *koinonia* (i.e., fellowship) language of St. Paul in 1 Corinthians. I have no problem with this. It is perfectly apt and also life giving.

ID: Like you, I also embrace the *koinonia* language of St. Paul in 1 Corinthians. We stand on solid ground here when we see the church as a fellowship of diversity and difference following Christ and living into what God has called us to be in the world. Once again here, for me (and maybe not for the drafters of the Windsor Report) I would want us to be careful when we speak of *koinonia* as the body of Christ and not necessarily the institution of the church.

I am particularly appreciative of the missiological overtones of the opening section of the Windsor Report and its invitation to consider Ephesians and 1 Corinthians in such a light. Here the key clarification is made that the church does not exist for itself but rather for the healing love of God in the world. Communion is not the end but rather a gift of the Trinitarian God for the sake of God's reconciling mission in the world. As the old civil rights song goes, "Keep your eyes on the prize." So I say hallelujah to the report's starting point that "The unity of the church, the communion of all its members with one another (which are the primary subjects of this report), and the radical holiness to which all Christ's people are called, are thus rooted in the Trinitarian life and purposes of the one God. They are designed not for their own sake (as though the church's in-house business were an end in itself), but to serve and signify God's mission to the world, that mission whereby God brings to men and women, to human societies and to the whole world, real signs and foretastes of that healing love which will one day put all things to rights" (par. 3). And again: "Paul would want to remind us of the unique source of that unity, our common identity in Christ, and its unique purpose, the furtherance of God's mission within the world" (par. 5). And let the people say Amen. Now if only the report kept its eyes on such a prize.

PZ: The authors of the report are inclined to offer theological conservatives considerable encouragement in underlining the Scriptures as core to Anglican self-understanding and belief. The authority of the Bible for the Communion is several times underlined. The problem, however, is that too much ground is given for interpreting variously texts in the Bible, such as those addressing homosexuality, which are unmistakable and clear. The report seems not to allow for the Bible's speaking with verbal and unchanging force and authority on a given question. Thus, "it must be seen that the purpose of Scripture is not simply to supply true information, nor just to prescribe in matters of belief and conduct, nor merely to act as a court of appeal, but to be part of the dynamic life of the Spirit. . . . Scripture is thus part of the means by which God directs the Church in its mission . . . " (sec. B, par. 55).

I find this sort of language to be completely inadequate in the present context of extreme difficulty for the church. It takes away with the left hand what the right hand has given. Note the bias against "true information," against "prescribe"-ing, against the idea of the Bible as a "court of appeal." Note the words "part of" in the last sentence. Most Evangelicals will be uncomfortable with this. It seems to reflect a fairly consistent ambiguity in the document.

ID: As to the authority of the Bible given by the Windsor Report, I believe that this is one of the strongest aspects of the report. Perhaps you and I get along so well because we both hold Holy Scripture as "containing all things necessary for salvation." I appreciate the unequivocal statement in the report that Holy Scripture "is recognized as the Church's supreme authority, and as such ought to be seen as a focus and means of unity" (par. 53).

But, if I read you correctly, we are not so much in the same camp with respect to the way that authority and biblical interpretation interact. I appreciate the report's statement that "the purpose of scripture is not simply to supply true information, not just to prescribe in matters of belief and conduct, nor merely to act as a court of appeal, but to be part of the dynamic life of the Spirit through which God the Father is within the world and in and through human beings. Scripture is thus part of the means by which God directs the Church in its mission [I would say in God's mission], energizes it for that task, and shapes and unites it so that it may be both equipped for this work and itself part of the message" (par. 55). I see this hermeneutical approach as thoroughly orthodox and thoroughly Anglican. We could do with more of this perspective across the Anglican Communion, in my opinion.

PZ: I am aware that church documents, and definitely Anglican documents, historically strive to reconcile and even unify diverging opinions. But this time, in the present crisis, we need at least a few absolute statements, both to affirm and reassure.

In short, the biblical foundations of the Windsor Report are too nuanced. This is to say, they concede too much to a contemporary distrust, in the West, of propositional truth.

ID: So, I guess, you and I then will have to agree to disagree, as to whether the texts in the Bible dealing with homosexuality are "unmistakable and clear." Please do not misunderstand me here, I am not arguing that there is a mandate in the Bible for same-sex relations. I simply do not see such. But on the other hand I do not see the prohibitions as strongly as you do, especially in light of other biblical prohibitions the Bible speaks to, such as divorce or how we are to handle our money (both of which the church has interpreted in various ways over the years).

Now as much as I appreciate the fact that the Windsor Report begins with the authority of Scripture, and then goes on to talk about the role of biblical interpretation within the community of the church, I am not at all sanguine about who the report seems to emphasize as the final arbiters of scriptural interpretation, namely, bishops and primates. While I wince at the slam of "academic researchers" in paragraph 58, I do not subscribe to the presentation that bishops (in the diocese) and primates (in the Communion) are the "accredited leaders" of the church who are in charge of biblical interpretation. This smacks of a kind of monarchical, representative presentation of bishops and primates that I do not think is Anglican (or at least is not American Episcopalian). Yes, bishops are teachers and have a special role in helping the gathered community to understand and interpret what God is saying in Holy Scripture, in a flat, mutually discerning, truth-seeking manner. But accreditation reeks of a power over, "I'm right because I am the bishop" form of episcope (pastoral oversight). I hope we can return to this presentation of the nature of bishops, because I think there will be much upon which we can agree here.

PZ: This is very good, Ian. We are basically agreed on some fundamental points here. You may judge Ephesians to be a little more copacetic to your sense of "church" than I, and I may believe that the Bible as a whole is "unmistakable" in its word on the question of homosexual practice. But in general, we are breaking through in this section!

Especially I am in full and even enthusiastic accord with your concern that the report gives too heavy a weight to bishops and presbyters as arbiters of the Scripture, that the report is monarchical *in potentia*. I wish to argue as a "low churchman" on this side of it, being wary of giving back to the institution what the Reformers very properly took away in favor of the missional laity. Your and my instincts, as Anglicans, in fact run counter to the tendency of the report to give a very large dose of authority and profile to bishops. Experience has taught us, or at least me, that this approach can easily slip over to arrogance on the part of the episcopate and infantilism on the part of the laity. I even agreed with Gene Robinson the other day on National Public Radio when he argued for a more democratic approach to our

ECUSA affairs than the Windsor Report allows. Here's to the Fourth of July!

ID: Ditto here, my friend.

What is the interpretive framework used in these sources? What hermeneutics are afoot?

PZ: The hermeneutical or interpretive framework used in treating the biblical sources that are brought forward by the document is a little deceptive. On the one hand, much is made of the centrality of Scripture in the church's making authoritative decisions concerning contested questions. On the other hand, there is a call here "to the whole Anglican Communion to re-evaluate the ways in which we have read, heard, studied and digested scripture" (sec. B.61). Moreover, much is made of "the bewildering range of available interpretative strategies and results" in handling Scripture (B.62)

The implication is that you more or less have to hold a doctoral degree in order to know what the Bible says about anything. You have to run everything through a big sieve, which is the mass of questions of context, intention, counter-text, the history of prior interpretation, present-day science and impressions, etc., in order to be able to say anything clear.

Now what lies behind this, I suspect, is the extreme unease with the passages in the Bible, especially the big one, Romans 1, which contest very definitely and explicitly the "practice" or exercise of homosexual relations. It has often been thought that the best way to get around these passages, and their incontestable unanimity, would be to argue to death their supporters with masses of interpretive filters by which it could be concluded that they do not mean what they say. I think that the Windsor Report, while plainly affirming the centrality of the Bible, is again just a bit seeming to take back with the left hand what the right hand has given.

To the good, much is made of "reception," which is the idea that time eventually separates falsehood from truth in contested matters. But that is only in relation to matters which are not already crystal clear. Thus it is often argued that the question of the ordination of women to the priesthood, concerning which both sides of the question can be argued, almost equally, from the Bible, is a matter for reception. If Scripture, in other words, speaks with forked tongue, then time and use will end up determining the thing. I agree with that.

But I do not agree with it in the case of homosexuality. In this presenting issue, the texts are too unanimously clear. So I therefore get nervous when the Windsor Report makes much of nuance and "complexity," for I believe it is exactly that kind of word which will prove the Trojan Horse for exactly what we have seen already happen in ECUSA — which is the blithe ordination of a gay bishop over the protest of the entire world's Christian community.

ID: Maybe this is a cop-out here, but I think I have responded already to this in our discussion of the previous question.

PZ: Yes, I think that is perhaps a cop-out. Because you have not countered on the question of hermeneutic, which says, I think, that the homosexuality issue is in a different sector than, say, the question of the ordination of women to the priesthood, because the latter issue is answered *variously* in the Bible, while the former one is discussed with only one result. This really is a point. There are so many things in Scripture that can come out one or two or even three ways. Predestination, for example, can be argued both pro and con from the same New Testament. Certain questions concerning the divine attributes can be looked at from differing points of view as you page through the Bible.

But not this one! In this case, the burden of proof is on the people who wish to change the inherited teaching. And I want to know — I really want to know — what you will do, Ian, with the unanimity of the drift here. It is a Continental Drift, and not a tendency. And I do think — but with sympathy — that you have in fact done what you admit you have done, which is . . . duck!

Incidentally, I duck things all the time.

ID: Perhaps, I have, in fact, ducked the question here. Fair enough, I stand accused. I am in agreement with you that the biblical record, if you take it at face value, is pretty clear on homosexuality. That presupposes that the definitions of homosexuality in the minds of the biblical writers and in the current experience of good and faithful Christians are one and the same. I am not convinced that they are. Also, I think that there are other clear injunctions in the Bible that Christians, in different places and at different times, have departed from the strict letter of the law. I think, for example, of the matter of divorce. I guess what I am looking for is the same kind of open hermeneutic for understandings and questions related to homosexuality. I think that this is a thoroughly Anglican approach to Scripture and is what the Windsor Report espouses. And yes, those who would argue for a new understanding of homosexuality in the church do need to do our homework.

What authority does Scripture have?

PZ: Well, first, someone on the "right" of this question has to try to explain "why" we give so much deference to the Bible. It is easy to say that the Bible comes first, followed by tradition and then by human reason in that order. And it is easy to say that the Bible should always win, if church tradition or if human reason goes counter to what it says. And I believe that. I will always seek to put the Bible incontestably in first place whenever and if ever its voice is challenged by any other voice.

But why? Why attach such heavy weight to this single, albeit important text? Why personally would I go to that length? And especially why go to such lengths, if one will thereby be associated with Southern Baptists and the people who supposedly gave George Bush his big win in November 2004? If guilt by association means anything at all, one would be a whole lot better off giving the Bible a miss, especially in the fatally un-PC assertion that the gay lifestyle is in fact a bad and damaging thing for the human being.

Why do I lend so much force and weight to the Scripture? It is because the Scripture contains the gospel! The Scripture contains the Word from outside ourselves that, to quote the African American steel-guitar spiritual, "God is a good God, yes he is." I am so enthralled, and finally helped and saved, by the good news of God's graceful pardon and new birth to sinners that I will seek to credit it anywhere I hear it. And I hear that message of Grace most powerfully and densely in the Bible.

Ian, I am not a fundamentalist. I am not one who believes that every sentence and every word of the Bible is equally valuable, or even equally God's Word. There are a few sentences in 2 Peter that make me cringe. Also a verse or two of Hebrews. I have less of a problem with "heavy law" passages in the Old Testament, as those, I believe, will almost all lead me to Christ's Grace, as the Law always does. I do not use the Bible as Islam usually uses the Qur'an. Islam normally views the Qur'an as equally endowed with authority in every single inspired word and every inspired verse. I do not understand the Bible that way.

ID: Paul, neither you nor I are into "Bibliolatry." I would never ever accuse you of being "fundamentalist." Neither would I accuse you of that other loaded epitaph that is often leveled across the chasm between different views of what the Bible says about homosexuality, namely, "homophobe." There is much opportunity for repentance on "both sides of the aisle" when it comes to the hurling of hurtful names at each other. So I am so pleased we are not going there.

PZ: Ian, that is a very happy paragraph you have written. Neither of us is a "fundamentalist." Neither of us is a "homophobe." And that clearing the air is really a terrific thing. People often label me as both. It is the absolute kiss of death in Christian community and fellowship. Those words are so negative and so opprobrious, that once they are leveled at you, you can almost never recover. So thank you, really *thank you*, for setting those demons to rest.

ID: Paul, I am so sorry that you and others who hold your position on questions related to homosexuality have been slandered in the past and continue to be so today in some corners. Likewise, I have had some pretty difficult epithets and mistruths hurled at my colleagues and me too. All of which, on both sides, are terribly hurtful and completely un-Christian. I hope and pray that what we are about in this discussion is that we are modeling a different kind of conversation, a different kind of being in communion. Even if nobody takes our positions on sexuality and ecclesiology seriously, I do hope that those listening in will see a different kind of Christian charity and love in our conversation, a charity and love that builds up the Body rather than tearing it apart. We can ask for no more.

Now that we have that established, let me say that I have no problem with your presentation of Scripture as primary when it comes to the threefold (and not fourfold — adding experience) formularies of Anglican theological method (sometimes known as Hooker's three-legged stool). In my mind, the stool does not sit flat, but rather there is an ordered way (different length legs if you will) by which we as Anglicans bring Scripture, Reason, and Tradition to bear on vexing questions before the church. I want to correct you a bit and say that at least in Richard Hooker's mind the order is Scripture, Reason, and Tradition and not Scripture, Tradition, and Reason. "What Scripture doth plainly deliver, to that the first place of credit and obedience is due: the next whereunto, is what any man can necessarily conclude by force of reason; after this, the voice of the church succeedeth" (Richard Hooker, *Laws of Ecclesiastical Polity.* Book V, 8:2). Here I would argue that when it seems that the Body of Christ is having some significant disagreement over the meaning of Scripture on a particular question (which I think is happening across the Anglican Communion with respect to questions of homosexuality), then we need to see what contributions our Reason can bring to the question. So I think the Windsor Report is spot on in its challenge to the Episcopal Church to articulate how we have arrived at where we are in the Episcopal Church with respect to our decisions of General Convention 2003 (par. 60 and 135).

PZ: Let me acknowledge my mistake in handling Hooker's three-legged stool. It is Scripture, Reason, then Tradition. That actually sounds awfully good to these Protestant ears. And I almost want to page Peter Gomes, who is also a dear friend and who has written some very similar things. So yes, I was wrong on the secondary and tertiary order, and am glad to know this.

From there I can go quite a ways with the first sections of the Windsor Report, which will not equate the written word with the Word Made Flesh in Christ Himself. The Bible, in other words, is not one of the Persons of the Trinity. Bibliolatry is therefore not a notion with which we, most Anglican Evangelicals, and "traditionalists" in general, are comfortable.

But we have come to a fountain, the Fountain Fill'd with Blood, and we find this Fountain uniquely opened up in the Scriptures. So we are very, very reluctant to second-guess the "package." We are quite unprepared to deconstruct the document which has brought us the word from outside ourselves, which is the Word of divine Grace to strugglers and criminals.

ID: I think it is worthwhile, however, considering how the Episcopal Church and our process of theological discernment is different from that of some other churches in the Anglican Communion, specifically the Church of England. Whereas the C of E, when it begins to wrestle with difficult concerns, commissions a blue-ribbon study of academic-minded bishops on whatever the question at hand is, the Episcopal Church goes about business through a more legislative and democratic political process. Consider the questions of sexuality before the church today. The Church of England tackled the issue head-on intellectually and theologically in its tightly argued and well-presented 358-page report *Some Issues in Human Sexuality*. The English penchant for understatement never ceases to amaze me. They produce 358 pages on such wide-ranging topics as heterosexuality, homosexuality, bisexuality, and "transexuality" and call it "some issues." I wonder what a comprehensive discussion of issues would look like to the Church of England?

To find the same level of engagement with these issues of human sexuality in the Episcopal Church, one could not pull a volume off of the shelf like *Some Issues in Human Sexuality* but would have to do a search of the commission reports, legislative committee hearings, and General Convention resolutions going back decades. All of this is to say that the Episcopal Church has indeed done much work on questions of sexuality through the years, and if one were to mine the resources in our common deliberative and legislative record, one could find a relatively coherent and well-articulated sense of how we got to where we are. Now if the Episcopal Church is to be faithful to what the Windsor Report is calling for, we will go back and collect this common deliberative and legislative data and make it available for the wider Communion. Such would also go a fair bit down the road of helping our sisters and brothers in Christ around the Communion understand how different our polity structures are and can be. And mind you, we too need to learn about how other churches around the Anglican Communion go about discerning what God would have them do on thorny issues.

PZ: Recently, I had written a manuscript, the final edit of which proved disturbing to me, its original author. The proofreader of the book had way exceeded her brief, as proofreader, and had edited the text in an interventionist manner. Hundreds of supposed corrections to what I had written proved to be attacks on the content. I complained to the publisher. What was at stake was the voice of the author. It was just so important that the person who had composed the book be able to say that what he had written would be what people would read. Let them, the readers, then decide what they think. But don't second-guess the original writer.

In an infinitely more significant sphere, we have to let the Bible stand. This is because time and tradition and our own wracked personal experience of being saved in defeating impasse after impasse in this vale of tears have inevitably and with astonishing completeness confirmed the Bible's truth. "Don't Mess with Bill!" (The Marvelettes).

ID: So, returning to the real question as you see it, it seems that the real dividing point between us is that you see the Bible as clear and unambiguous on questions of homosexuality and I do not. In Hooker's terms, you see "Scripture doth plainly delivering" on questions of homosexuality and I do not. As I said before, I grant you the fact that I do not find in the Bible a commendation of homosexuality. But the prohibitions against such are no more clear and unambiguous to me than other difficult issues with which the church has had to wrestle. Does this mean that the matter of the place of gay and lesbian Christians in the life of the church is settled, once and for all? Obviously not. And I'm not convinced that the process of "reception" by which the church comes to agreement on questions of homosexuality will be completed one way or the other in our lifetimes. The question thus is this: how are we going to live together, or why should we live together, in the meantime?

PZ: On the question of the difference between the Church of England's approach to theological arbitration and our own — I mean, ECUSA's — I have to leave that to you to some extent, as you know the recent history much better than I do. I have always received both churches' approach as relatively verbose and even dithering. You want to establish a clear difference in the way the American Church has declared itself, more or less, on this issue. *Ça suffit!* But I would still rather rest my case, as a whole, on the Scriptures, as a whole. And that does not mean disregarding human science and reason and reflection. But only in, as you rightly say, second place.

ID: On the way that the Episcopal Church (and even the C of E) get at theological questions, I have no problem with our processes being "relatively verbose and even dithering." But hey, I am less taken with the clarity of the Reformation than you are. Call me messy and fuzzyheaded, and I will not argue with you.

What do these biblical sources say about the specifics of the crisis in the Anglican Communion?

PZ: Well, I think the real biblical sources say what needs to be said right up front now, but is not said in the report: that St. Paul oddly fixes on an ancient prohibition regarding the practice of same-gender sexual loving as a form of narcissism, which in his view constitutes idolatry. This is very heavy of Paul, and in a real way surprising. Why should he, the exponent of God's Grace ne plus ultra, have decided to single out, as it were, homosexuality from the traditional Jewish index of sins? I am sure we almost all wish he had not done so. As I have said before, it would have made it a lot easier on a great many people. It certainly would have lightened my own career path in the Episcopal Church! It would have saved a big run on the Church Pension Fund. It would have probably saved a whole lot of wear and tear in families and with siblings and between parents and children, and even between wives and husbands.

But Paul did, nevertheless, focus on this one thing. And he deepened the focus quite powerfully, attaching the charge of narcissism — loving the same, rather than loving the other — to it. I want to say that the biblical sources of the New Testament have a *lot* to say about the specifics of the crisis in the Anglican Communion. But the Eames Commission is not saying this. The Commission is not saying it at all.

ID: Okay, Paul, you are giving me the bait here, but I'm afraid I'm not going to take it. I'm not going to try and explain away Paul's prohibition regarding the practice of same-gender sexual relations. Neither am I going to go where I think you want to go, namely, your challenge that we should not duck what you consider the real issue of what the Bible says about homosexuality. I just do not share your passion or commitment for such a discussion/debate.

Now, I want to own here that my privilege as a heterosexual, legally and happily married man (thanks be to God for the gift of my wife and our partnership) lets me off of the hook of having to engage personally questions of the place of gay and lesbian people in the church and in wider society. And perhaps I am not being the good ally to those who are struggling for the full acceptance of gay and lesbian people in the life of the church, but I simply do not see the benefit of single-identity politics. As long as we are fighting over one particular issue, be it human sexuality, race, class, gender, etc., then it is way too easy to construct winners and losers, who is in and who is out, who is right and who is wrong (on both sides of the question). When this happens we will always be divided along whatever single axis we choose. It is only when we begin to see each other in the fullness of how God has created us that we will be able to see how each and every one of us both share some fundamental attributes that unite us and some fundamental attributes that divide us, all at the same time. Our unity with each other and with God will not be discovered if we are comparing and contrasting each other in a hierarchical comparison of any single oppression or privilege. Rather our unity is discovered in the fact that each and every one of us both has points of brokenness and hurt on one side, and points of privilege and gifts on the other. Our unity then is found in the fullness of what God has created in our many differences and not in any one battle over single-identity politics.

You do, however, raise an important point in your discussion of St. Paul's take on homosexuality, namely, the charge of narcissism. Many in the Anglican Communion, especially those of us in the United States who can afford to, live as if we are the center of the universe and only our reality matters. This is definitely something of which we need to repent. There is nothing worse than thinking and behaving that one is the end-all and be-all, and that everything we represent is good and right, while all that the other is, is bad and wrong. I'm afraid that in Anglicanism today, both in the Episcopal Church and across the Anglican Communion, there is entirely way too much vilification of the other informed by our narcissistic need to be right.

PZ: Yes, Ian, you didn't take the bait, but then you sort of did. You want to say that the argument over homosexuality involves an inevitable win-lose contest, with an almost arbitrary result. You postulate that we are all broken, on whatever front we are broken, and that to peer at this particular area, i.e., homosexuality, is no different than to peer at any other. I agree with you! We are all utterly and indelibly and impermeably broken — and that is the starting point for all Christian experience as I see it. I just don't want us as Anglican Christians to get away from that insight: that whether it is homosexuality or heterosexuality, everything is affected and implicated in Original Sin, which is just another way of saying the *conditio humana*. My problem all along with the gay community's argument is that it wants to say that anything un-chosen is therefore by definition not under judgment. *That,* and that almost alone, is my problem with the argument I almost always hear repeated so vehemently, to wit, how can God condemn me for something I did not choose?

But that view of choice, which I think is an American heresy, mistakes the profoundest part of the Christian understanding of Original Sin: that our humanity is responsible even for what we have not chosen but simply are. This is for me the big question.

The Commission is making a conscious end run around the whole real and material question that is before it. This is why I said earlier that we should not duck the real issue. My main problem with the Windsor Report is the same problem I have with so many of these exercises: they are exercises in process, not in substance. I remember what Noam Chomsky says about the "Peace Process" in the Middle East. It is a "process" designed *not* to bring peace. It is a way of putting off "peace," in the interests of other agendas, while somehow saying it is not doing that. So my main problem with the Eames Commission is that it dwells on process rather than substance.

And because later in the report the cue is given that its recommendations are to give a stasis "until" the Communion has a chance to reconsider the question or enlarge its mind concerning sexuality, I believe that the total emphasis of the Commission on matters of "process" rather than substance gives away an improper open-endedness to a question that is not up for discussion. Like Ulster in 1916, "Scripture has decided."

Now back to the biblical sources which the document does import — as opposed to the more important sources which the document neglects to touch. The main sources used are Ephesians, for its high view of the church, and 1 Corinthians, for its teaching about the Body of Christ and also its teaching about "adiaphora" (i.e., nonessentials). I myself would have sourced more "low church" sources such as Galatians and 2 Corinthians, which always subordinate the church to the Holy Spirit, not to mention to the teaching of the Grace and Justification that come from God. I also would have listed Paul's teaching on homosexuality to be under essentials rather than adiaphora. I would also have wanted to underline the "cheap grace" teaching that the political forces behind the consecration of Gene Robinson bring out again and again. I would have wished to focus on the required character of repentance in Christian life — as opposed to "regret," but more on that distinction below — and the moral self-effacement to which the Cross always summons a person and communities.

Ephesians allows the interpreter to speak too cosmologically concerning "unity" as such. I would have wished to temper this with the orthodox atonement teaching of Colossians and 1 Peter.

But again, my main point is that the Commission right from the starting line took its mandate as *only* to deal with issues of "communion," which are formal questions in the philosophical sense, rather than with issues of moral theology, which are material questions in the same sense. This was the fatal hour. Rachel is thus crying for her children, and she will not be comforted.

ID: I guess then that I am fully in the camp of the Lambeth Commission Report in dwelling on what you consider "process rather than substance." As long as we are fighting over questions of sexuality in the Anglican Communion, I do not see any way out. Someone is bound to win and someone is bound to lose. So for me, I'd rather go where the Windsor Report goes, namely, what is the nature of Communion and how is it that we as Anglicans are going to stay together in the midst of these difficult issues?

PZ: What I do like here about what you are saying is that you *are* talking about substance and not just process. All we are asking, to quote John Lennon, is "give peace a chance" — i.e., talk with us "conservatives" about what we are really interested in, which is substance more than process, the meaning of peace and not just "road maps" to peace.

ID: Yes, Paul, substance is key, and I'm more than willing to discuss substance here. I have always appreciated your very high embrace of the atonement. I agree that the human condition is one of sinfulness and that Christ's victory on the cross is very basic to salvation. That having been said, I take the atoning sacrifice of Jesus on the cross as part of the whole wonderful mystery of what God did in the birth, life, death, resurrection, and ascension of Jesus as incarnate God. I do not, as you might, privilege Jesus' death as any higher than or any more important than his birth, his life and ministry, his resurrection, and his ascension. For me the saving work of God in Jesus is the whole deal, not simply the atonement. Perhaps I've misjudged your Christology here. If I have, I apologize and would like to be corrected.

As to how you characterize the view that "the gay community's argument is that it wants to say that anything unchosen is therefore by definition not under judgment," I'm afraid I simply do not see such. It is true that there are some in the "gay community" and in the "heterosexual community" in the Episcopal Church who might not share our understanding of the sinfulness of the *conditio humana* and thus our commitment to the atoning work of Jesus. But I do not see folk arguing that because something is not chosen it is thus free from sin. That is exactly why advocates for the public Rites of Blessing for same-sex unions (at least in the legislative record of the Episcopal Church) want to hold same-sex covenanted relationships to the standards of loving, monogamous, lifelong, chaste, and faithful mutuality. Sin being what it is, it infects all of our lives whether heterosexual or homosexual.

What do the sources say about the nature of God?
The nature of the Church? The nature of communion?

ID: Section B of the Windsor Report opens with what I find to be a wonderful expression of the nature of communion. The emphasis on Communion as from God expressed in relationship through "bonds of affection" is particularly well done here. The report emphasizes that Communion is primarily about relationship with God, "who is himself a communion of Father, Son and Holy Spirit" (par. 45). As much as we are bound to the Trinitarian God through our baptism we are also bound to each other through the relational love of God. There is a wonderful embrace of the mutuality of relations with God and with each other that harkens back to the great offering of the 1963 Anglican Congress in Toronto, "Mutual Responsibility and Interdependence in the Body of Christ," or MRI for short. MRI gave Anglicans a vision for the church that saw us all as equals, bound together in a common life with the Trinitarian God and with each other. Part of the problem that I think we have gotten ourselves into as Anglicans today is that we have lost some of the vision of mutuality and interdependence that was given to us those four decades ago in Toronto. And I believe that MRI and the 1963 Anglican Congress actually resulted in a roadmap for communion that has been more constructive and forward looking than any structure or "instrument of unity" has.

Thus here at the beginning of Section B, I find a helpful and positive presentation of the relational nature of communion. "Communion is, in fact, all about mutual relationships. It is expressed by community, equality, common life, sharing, interdependence, and mutual affection and respect. It subsists in visible unity, common confession of the apostolic faith, common belief in scripture and creeds, common baptism and shared Eucharist, and a mutually recognized ministry. Communion means that each church recognizes that the other belongs to the One, Holy, Catholic and Apostolic Church of Jesus Christ, and shares in the whole mission of God" (par. 49). There is sense here that the communion we share, the communion which is at the heart of the Trinity and is from God, is best lived into when we come together in a common Eucharistic fellowship that empowers us for service to the mission of God. I celebrate the liturgical, missiological trajectory here. Would that these trajectories had been further developed in the report, but I'm afraid that they are not.

In light of this understanding, the Anglican Communion for me is a Eucharistic fellowship of churches that share a common history and inheritance with roots in the Church of England, including the ancient Celtic and Saxon churches of the British Isles (par. 47). The raison d'être of this communion of churches is to serve and advance God's mission of reconciliation, restoration, and renewal in a hurting, broken, and sinful world. "Our communion enables us, in mutual interdependence, to engage in our primary task, which is to take forward God's mission to his needy and much loved world" (par. 46).

PZ: This second chapter of ours, Ian, is perhaps giving too much airtime to the relatively brief attention given in the document to Scriptural sources as such. The report tends to divide the authority of the exalted Christ from the authority of the written Word, which is inevitably to downplay the plain literary sense of the written Word. In other words, the cosmological Christology of Ephesians can be used to subordinate the Bible to the One of whom the Bible speaks. Fair enough. But this should not be a Trojan Horse by which is imported a lower view of the authoritative "holy law" of the Old and New Testaments than most of us on the "traditional" side are able to accept.

We all owe Luther much for distinguishing between the Christ who is Mary's son, from the "manger," i.e., the Bible, that holds Him yet to our gaze and ears. But Luther's distinction could be used to devolve the massive inherited authority of the written Word. I do not wish to demote in any way the plain sense of the plain words we have been given.

On the church, the emphasis of the Body of Christ passages of the New Testament can be taken in a "catholic" direction to say that the Body of Christ is the church visible and institutional. I seem to be hearing that argument from a lot of ECUSA bishops these days. As in, how can you distinguish the Christ from His Body here on earth? Or to put it more in the vernacular, love Him, love His Church! (And I, your bishop, embody His Church. . . .)

In principle, I do not accept this. Not for a New York minute. Organic or physical unity — unity of communion in the material sense — should be trumped by apostolic truth. In every case. Organic unity for its own sake creates fascism. And fascism in the church means prelacy, control, focus on structure rather than foundation. This is what if anything we need to resist. So I am unpersuaded by the report's placing of weight on unity in visual or formal terms at the potential expense of unity in theological and propositional terms.

It is true that the report's aspiration, indeed hunger, for the persistence of communion between and among different churches or provinces that see things differently in some key areas is a noble and excellent thing. And certainly our approach to adiaphora makes such communion possible over wide swaths of difference and custom and tradition and history. But among things that are not adiaphora — and many of us conceive of this particular teaching on homosexuality that ECUSA is avouching as being not of the adiaphora, but touching on the darkest, deepest questions of the problem of being human and the divine Christian response to it — organic communion will not hold.

So again, I am uncomfortable with the cut that is made in the document between the authoritative God in Christ and the authoritative Word from that God in Christ. I am uncomfortable with the overly vertical view of the church on earth, which the report projects in its earliest sections. And I am uncomfortable with the sense that communion could hold undamaged, barring only sins against the Trinity or the Incarnation.

ID: Now while affirming this grand missiological vision of communion at the beginning of Section B, I — like you, Paul — am a little skeptical of what seems to be a sometimes inflated view of the church. I like the distinction that I think you are making between the "authority of the exalted Christ and the authority of the written Word." You have convinced me, the good Protestant that you are, that the Windsor Report tends to a more "vertical" view of the church. And yes, I agree with you that when we start moving away from the authority of the written Word (and its call to God's mission, I would add) and placing all of our trust in the authority of the "exalted Christ," then this opens up possible abuses of authority by the church. And so I am in agreement with your "vernacular" cautionary description of "love Him, love His Church, and I, your bishop, embody His Church" as an operating ecclesiology in the report.

I do not think that what you are saying here about the nature of episcopacy is too over the top. While I do agree that the episcopate helps to express the unity of the Communion, I do not see it as "putting into effect" the unity of the Communion (par. 63). Bishop as sign and symbol of the unity that God has given us in the Body of Christ, yes, but bishop as the agent that brings into being our unity through some kind of representative function, this is not for me. And I'm not convinced that the representative (dare I say monarchical) view of the episcopate is not entirely Anglican either, at least not American Episcopalian. So I am not comfortable with the statement that "Bishops represent the universal Church to the local and vice versa" (par. 64). And I am even less at ease with the supporting footnote to this statement, "Bishops represent Christ to the people, but also bring the people and their prayers to God" (footnote 38). The fact that this "representative" view of the episcopate occurs on a couple of occasions in the report, paragraph 64/footnote 38 and again in paragraph 124/footnote 81, is worrisome. This becomes increasingly problematic when the representative view of the episcopate is elevated even further when the report considers the nature of primacy and the Primates Meeting. We can take this up again later.

PZ: Ian, we seem both to be hearing that song from *Iolanthe* by Gilbert and Sullivan. Remember it?: "The Law is the very embodiment / of everything that's excellent. / It has no kind of fault or flaw, / and I, my Lords, embody the Law." You and I are hearing something of that tone in the parts of the report that want to depict bishops as God's utter gift to the cosmos.

You and I *are* Episcopalians. That is, we honor bishops as the focal point of our unity and of our teaching and of our family fellowship as sisters and brothers. But we do not see bishops as a sort of Jacob's Ladder to the heavenlies. That is to give them a power and a weight that is beyond their brief and beyond our human need. Bishops are not, in other words, the present incarnation of Jesus Christ.

There are two other points here in which we agree utterly. First, we agree that the church is a horizontal organism in its practical outworking. It embodies those "bonds of affection" which we cherish. Yes, it is also more than that, but only in its Referent, not so much in its institutional life. Its institutional life is horizontal, in other words, not vertical. This, we believe, is what the American Church tried to maintain after the Revolutionary War. It was, as it were, a democratic vision for Anglicanism. Ian, were you there — it was in Philadelphia, I think, at an Episcopal Church Foundation colloquium — when our colleague Eugene Lowe sought in a lecture to understand the roots of the Episcopal Church polity? He blamed it on Philadelphia! Seriously, he saw in Bishop White's very nonprelatical vision of the church the origins of the autonomous idea of Anglicanism that took root here after 1781. I think that is something of what you and I are talking about, and agreeing about. We are just a little cautious concerning that aspect of the Windsor Report which understands bishops, and primates, to be the defining as well as the disciplining organ of the church.

Now it is true that people on the "Gene Robinson side," as it were, could at this particular point in history delightedly lunge towards a less prelatical model of the church in defense of our American right to go our own way. (Isn't the state motto of New Hampshire, "Live Free or Die"?) It *could* be that in their haste to defend the right of one of our dioceses, not to mention ECUSA as a whole, to do its own thing, in this particular department, the early history of American Episcopalianism could be a sort of tool of expediency to "cover" a specific controversial decision. I hope this is not what is happening. But I do want to run and not walk to agree with you about our shared nervousness concerning bishops being the ultimate arbiter of anything.

The second point in which I find myself in fundamental agreement with you concerns the missional character of our church. We must remain a church that travels light, or at least is not top-heavy in its concept of authority. You are swift to emphasize the missionary *Vorrang* (priority) in Christianity. There again I am with you. And the Windsor Report could be a tilt towards a "heavier" and more vertical picture of authority. I don't mind a truly vertical picture of authority, as in Scripture and actually the revelation of the Word from the Cross, entirely from outside ourselves. But I am very wary of human authority — as in a churchmanship that concedes the whole enchilada to the Men in Purple. (Did you see *Men in Black*? They were the self-appointed guardians of the galaxy.)

ID: Paul, I love the way you pull in everything from Gilbert and Sullivan to *Men in Black* as you make allusions to what we see going on in the Anglican Communion. "Men in Purple as the self-appointed guardians of the galaxy" is just too good of an image. I'm afraid I'll never see a meeting of the House of Bishops or a Lambeth Conference in the same way again. Thanks so much.

Yes, I think we are in fundamental agreement here as to what we see as the high embrace of bishops as increasingly definitive of Anglican ecclesiology and authority today. If there is one take-home message from our conversation that I would like our listeners to have it, would be: We need to be very leery of the increasing centralization of authority in bishops that is happening in the Anglican Communion today. Full stop. Such is profoundly un-Anglican, at least in the history and experience of the United States and our sister and brother churches around the world who share our mission history and polity.

You and Gene Lowe are correct in your understanding that the idea that the people should check episcopal authority and power is a particular gift to Anglicanism from the Episcopal Church in the United States. Interestingly and relatedly, I believe, the Episcopal Church also gave to the Anglican Communion the whole idea of the missionary episcopate. Now, in missionary episcopate I do not mean the bishops who are currently crossing diocesan boundaries such as those sponsored by the Anglican Mission in America. Rather I mean the missionary bishops, the greats of the nineteenth and twentieth centuries such as Jackson Kemper for the Northwest of the United States and William J. Boone in China, who brought the church to places and people where it had not yet existed. There is something in the fact that "bishops by ballot" also leads to an understanding of the episcopate as first and foremost about mission. Too bad that the Windsor Report advances a hierarchical and representative view of bishops and not the latter, more democratic and missiological view of the episcopate.

PZ: Ian, the Episcopal Church that draws your willing obedience, as it does mine, is missional, democratic, laity-driven, and also, God willing, Resting in the Given, which is Christ on the Cross, the Word from outside ourselves per se.

What biblical motifs and passages are not included in the report? What do you think is missing and why?

PZ: I have already tried to say that Scripture's key passages concerning homosexuality are AWOL in the Windsor Report. You may immediately wish to say, Well, that was not the stated brief of the Commission. But I am still not convinced. How can we mark out a process if we have set our faces resolutely against the issue that ignited the blaze in the first place? It is not that I oppose the concept of looking at communion thoroughly in light of biblical ecclesiologies. But I do insist that ecclesiology is always second in importance to anthropology, Christology, and soteriology. Doctrines of the church need to flow out of core theology, and not be developed in some kind of parallel segregation from it. My objection to the Windsor Report is to its idée fixe, that the real question of the day is off-limits. Such a bracketing of the "problem" will end up not solving or resolving the problem.

ID: I am in agreement with your analysis that the Windsor Report does not address the topic of homosexuality directly. The report states clearly, however, that the "illness" in the Communion has been brought on by two key questions that are indeed related to the place of gay and lesbian people in the church. These questions are: "whether or not it is legitimate for the church to bless committed, exclusive and faithful relationships of same sex couples, and whether or not it is appropriate to ordain, and or consecrate to the episcopate persons living in a sexual relationship with a partner of the same sex" (par. 23). In this respect, the Lambeth Commission was very clear that the actions of the Diocese of New Westminster in the Anglican Church of Canada allowing for the blessing of same-sex unions, and the election of the Rt. Rev. V. Gene Robinson as Bishop of New Hampshire and consented to by the House of Deputies and Diocesan Bishops at General Convention in 2003, are the presenting facts that have called into question the nature of communion in the Anglican Communion. So yes, questions related to homosexuality are not far below the surface in the Windsor Report.

I do not agree with you, however, that the Commission should have taken on directly these questions about homosexuality. I am not convinced at all that an international commission in the Anglican Communion, even one that is truly representative of the many voices and positions in Anglicanism such as the Lambeth Commission was, could have come to any consensus on questions relating to the place of gay and lesbian Christians in the church. To suggest that an international Anglican commission could come to a reconciling, constructive, and unified offering in these very heady, difficulty, and polarized times in the Communion is unrealistic, I believe. I am also not convinced, as you seem to be, that the jury is out on blessing of same-sex unions and the ordination of gay and lesbian Christian leaders. As a result, I am very comfortable with the Lambeth Commission's clear mandate not to take on matters of human sexuality and their related position that *"serious Communion-wide discussion of the relevant issues* (related to human sexuality) *is clearly needed as a matter of urgency"* (par. 26, italics in the original).

PZ: In addition to a section on homosexuality itself, biblically considered, I would also have drawn on the Galatians 4 passage on the free woman and the slave woman, for its implications concerning "church." Also there are important passages in Acts where Spirit and "church" come into conflict; not to mention the vast implications of St. John's ecclesiology in his Gospel, by which the "chosen" ones almost always are in conflict with the truth, with the Truth. In other words, I would have wished to be more Protestant in my sense of what the church is and how soundly it can err, and become unsound, even at times embodying the wickedness in high places.

Jesus's attitude towards the Temple would also have been apposite. I sometimes wonder whether our big problem in ECUSA is not, in fact, "liberal" theology or "conservative" reaction to it; but rather prelacy, old-fashioned prelacy, which mistakes the visible for the invisible. For me, the diocesan bishops of ECUSA, who continue, many of them, to take a very hard line against those who cross geographical boundaries and those clergy who support the famous Network, may be the ones who are creating the problem. There is an impermeable ecclesiology to many of our diocesan leaders. They make loud noises to the effect that being uncanonical in relation to jurisdiction is as bad and worse, probably, than being un-catholic and un-apostolic in faith and morals.

I am becoming convinced, partly from my own experience traveling up and down this church, that a kind of bowing down to canon and central authorization defines the adversary, rather than the supporters of "the present incumbent of the see of New Hampshire." I am not sure that "Gene Robinson" is the problem. The problem is the ecclesiology of those who are playing hardball. In contrast, we need a New Testament ecclesiology that is permeable, flexible, nonlinear, nonhierarchical, and open to all manner of paradigms and models.

Here I can join forces with the most "liberal"-minded among us. As long as the Holy Spirit is unleashed out of the great shelter of Grace that is the Bible, I am happy for "the wind to list where it will." Ian, help me here. Do you agree?

ID: I believe you when you say that in your "own experience traveling up and down this church, that a kind of bowing down to canon and central authorization defines the adversary." Here I'm tempted to say that I'm glad that you give credence to the power of your experience (just a little joke, Paul). I do want to acknowledge, in a serious vein, that I, unlike you, am not in the target position of dissenting from the decisions of the 2003 General Convention. And so I want to offer my empathy and support to you when you say that you have found a bowing down to canon and central authorization as defining, while this has not been my experience in the Episcopal Church.

That having been said, I do think that in the broader Anglican Communion there is a growing "bowing down to canon and central authorization." I would argue that over the last couple of decades in the Anglican Communion, there has been an increasing tendency to a centralization of authority and power. And I'm afraid to say that there is much in the Windsor Report that heads in this direction. I'll go into this deeper as our discussion continues, as that is not the focus of our current question at hand. For the moment, let me stand shoulder to shoulder with you in the call for "a New Testament ecclesiology that is permeable, flexible, nonlinear, nonhierarchical, and open to all manner of paradigms and models" at home and in the wider Anglican Communion. To that end, I wish that the Windsor Report had lifted up Pentecost and the spread of the church empowered by the Holy Spirit in Acts. In the polyphonic and polycentric (as Professor Christopher Duraisingh, my colleague here at EDS, is quick to emphasize) reality of Pentecost we are invited into a permeable, open, multivocal ecclesiology. To me a Pentecost-informed ecclesiology makes a whole lot of sense for the "new Pentecost" we are living into in the multicultural, polyphonic reality of the contemporary Anglican Communion.

Before leaving this immediate discussion of Scripture, there is still one note I wish I had seen in the Windsor Report, and here I will talk like a missiologist (student of Christian mission) again. Most missiologists would agree that in order to comprehend what God is up to in the world, what God's mission is for the world (the *missio Dei*), what the role of the church is in God's mission, the whole of Scripture needs to be taken into consideration as one unified story of God's love for creation. One of the best examples of this is the wonderful presentation "From Creation to New Creation: The Mission of God in the Biblical Story" that your own Professor of Biblical Studies and Mission at Trinity, Professor Grant LeMarquand, made to the House of Bishops in September 2001.* Now I am sympathetic to the Windsor Report's caution against taking bits and pieces of Scripture out of context or using one or another verses as a kind of proof text. I just wish, however, that the report had emphasized the fact that the whole of Holy Scripture is primarily a missionary document about a missionary God whose mission it is to reconcile, restore, and renew a divided, broken, and fallen creation. Let our ecclesiology flow from our missiology, and let our missiology flow from the Grand Story of God in the whole of Holy Scripture.

PZ: Ian, this is good. We still disagree and will probably continue to disagree concerning the two presenting issues, same-sex blessings and the ordination of active homosexuals. And I still am not convinced that the observable fact that no representative Anglican commission is going to be able to come up with a consensus statement concerning homosexuality is *sufficient* in itself to prevent us from trying. This is simply because I value truth — in a propositional and pre-postmodern sense — and believe that to every question there is at least the possibility of a clear answer. So I disagree with you that we should not try to arrive at something

---

*In *Waging Reconciliation: God's Mission in a Time of Globalization and Crisis*, ed. Ian T. Douglas (New York: Church Publishing, Inc., 2002).

because the searchers are themselves impossibly conflicted before the search even begins. I understand why you think the Commission could not have striven for an answer to the "elephant in the living room," but that is not enough for me to believe that in principle they should not have tried. But now let's move forward despite our disagreement about the premise of the Commission.

ID: Yes, Paul, I think that you and I will have to disagree about the "two presenting issues, same-sex blessings and the ordination of active homosexuals." I think we will probably also have to disagree as to whether an international commission of the Anglican Communion can and should come up with a definitive position on questions related to homosexuality and the church. For I am not convinced that there is a good either/or solution to questions about sexuality before the Anglican Communion today. It's not that I do not value truth, I do. Perhaps I'm just a fuzzy-headed postmodernist, but I believe that in God's economy it is possible for seemingly mutually irreconcilable positions to coexist in a larger framework. For me the larger framework for these discussions about sexuality is our shared commitment to the gospel of Jesus Christ and the call to God's mission of reconciliation.

I think I have already said this, but it is worth repeating. The devil is not stupid. There is nothing more that the forces of evil want than for us Christians to become so embroiled in our inner-ecclesial infighting (as important as these issues are) that we neglect the larger call to God's work beyond the church. Because I believe the devil is not stupid and he will try to attack the places where good is most likely to be affected, I take the veracity with which we are tearing ourselves apart in Anglicanism as a sign that the Anglican Communion has never been better positioned to effect God's reconciling mission in the world. I consider the Decade of Evangelism, the leadership that Anglicans gave to pass international debt-relief legislation during the Clinton administration, and the current possibilities to fight the HIV/AIDS pandemic as genuine signs that the Anglican Communion has never before been so well positioned to serve God's mission in the world. So I am indeed hopeful for our peculiar family of churches.

PZ: What I continue to like and relate to in your replies is your inveterate wariness in relation to church centralization and hierarchical notions of authority. I take your wariness to derive from a high doctrine of the Spirit and also a warm investment in missional thinking. There I continue to be right with you. My teacher at Tübingen, Ernst Käsemann, always felt he discerned the decline in early church power and impact in the declination, even at the end of the first century, from St. Paul's very high doctrine (and experience) of the Holy Spirit. For Käsemann in his day, this meant "early catholicism": the retreat from substance (and also venturesomeness) to form (and structure). I still think Käsemann was right.

Recently a retired rector of the Church of England recounted how diocesan structures and centralizing control had weighed in very strongly and off-puttingly during the last, recent decade of his formal ministry. As a charismatic Evangelical (in C of E terms), he felt increasingly that his ministry was being monitored from outside and that big periods of his time were being taken up with paperwork and diocesan meetings and further diocesan meetings, and so on. He spoke from fatigue — and from the psychic fatigue arising from the mortmain of episcopal oversight in the negative sense.

I feel with this man. And like you, Ian, I see it in the Windsor Report. I see it in dioceses where I have served. And it is retarding our missional task, as you so rightly say.

So, Ian, we are arm in arm on the Holy Spirit and we are arm in arm on the centrality of Christian mission. That's a lot.

And I would like to add that this conversation is making me just a little more cautious of my own leaning on ideas of vertical authority (even when it agrees with other convictions of mine theologically) and a certain "high churchmanship" in service of orthodoxy. Do I, as a conservative in theology, really wish to tie my star to episcopal authority as such, even when it backs me? I am thinking "strange bedfellows," and all that. But perhaps I had better banish the thought!

Chapter 3

WHAT ABOUT THE CHURCH?

What is the Windsor Report saying about the nature of communion? "bonds of communion"? "bonds of affection"?

PAUL ZAHL: The report is saying that communion is both vertical and horizontal. It is vertical in that it concerns the common relation to God which all His children share. All Christians, in other words, are brothers and sisters because we relate to the one Father. Our horizontal equality and sibling relationship is organically fitted to our vertical relation to the same eternal Parent.

Communion is also more strictly horizontal because we are all, those to whom the report is addressed, considering ourselves "Anglican," that is, in communion with the tradition coming out of the English Christian Church, the Church of England. I am, for example, as an American Episcopalian, in communion with the Archbishop of Canterbury in England, and so is the confirmed member of the Diocese of North Ankole in Nigeria. Therefore the two of us, the Anglican from the Diocese of Pittsburgh and the Anglican from North Ankole, are in communion with one another. The verticality of communion is theological — we are both children of one divine Creator, Father, and Savior — and the verticality of communion is historical — we are both related, for reasons of history, to the Christian tradition as it came out of the Church of England.

IAN DOUGLAS: I like your imagery of the vertical and horizontal aspects of the nature of communion. Yes, I think that the verticality of communion is all about how we are united to the Creator God, through the life, death, and resurrection of Jesus Christ and how we are empowered in this relationship with God through the action of the Holy Spirit. So as long as the verticality is about relationship with the Triune God, through our common baptism, I'm good with that. We need to be careful, however, that the verticality not be interpreted in some kind of linear or hierarchical manner. Here I raise my concern once again about the monarchical presentation of the episcopacy that I find in the Windsor Report. The last thing I want in my vertical relationship with God is some office, or person, arbitrating or representing my relationship with God. So I am in accord with your sense of communion based on a vertical relationship with God, yet I want to exercise care and a certain hermeneutic of suspicion lest we stray into hierarchical and even patriarchical waters here.

PZ: We could really have no problems, either of us, with this under-standing of communion. It binds us each together, as well, even when we are wishing to differ about a disputed point in faith and morals. Our communion is, nevertheless, strained when the specific province of the communion of which we are both mem-ber, i.e., ECUSA, thumbs its nose formally and collectively at the larger body of sisters and brothers overseas. Then, the commu-nion is strained and begins to be stressed. And when ECUSA's thumbing of the nose occurs over a pretty important point — for me it is in the area of a church-dividing point — then the bonds of communion are attenuated almost to breaking point. It is at this breaking point that measures have to be taken. It is at this breaking point that a dysfunction needs to be "regretted," or bet-ter, apologized for, which is a weaker form of the controversial verb "repented of."

The expression "bonds of communion" expresses the vertical dimension of our church as that is worked out horizontally. I am bonded in communion with North Ankole, to use the ear-lier example, for theological and also historical reasons. These bring me together with the Christians of Ankole through an "ac-cident of birth" (i.e., British evangelical and church Christianity that is within my heritage and also within theirs). The accident of birth is the historical part. But I am also bonded in communion with the Anglican Christians in Ankole because we share explicitly the same Savior, the same Bible, the same God and Father of us all. We speak the same language. That is really true. We speak the same language. This is incidentally no less the language of Charles Simeon and even of Thomas Cranmer. It is probably not the same language spoken by David Jenkins, Richard Holloway, and possibly even any number of American bishops who voted conscientiously for the principle of having a gay bishop or approving same-sex unions. That is the rub. It is there where questions of substance — as in, what do we really think of this innovation in definite theological terms? rather than questions of process, how can I be in communion with someone who has a radically different theology of the religion itself? — become decisive. And it is here where the whole modus operandi of the Eames Commission is deficient. In any event, "bonds of communion" really do exist. But they are attenuated, like taffy at the beach, when the central values that founded and created them are not or no longer shared.

Now the term "bonds of affection" is a little different. I have affection towards Ian Douglas. Real affection, not manufactured (as in that awkward moment in so many Communion services which is called "The Peace"). I have a whole lot in common with Ian, plus also a shared history. And not only a shared history of some years now, but some shared history through hard times. We have shared, as it were, the stressful times of acute church conflict that have wracked us all in recent years. We have a shared history of — I hope this is not putting it too dramatically — suffering. "Liberals" have felt trashed and dismissed by "conservatives." Gay people in the church especially have a history of rejection and hurt. At the same time, "conservatives," like myself, have felt marginalized for many years. We are pretty emotional and fairly unworldly. We do not do church politics very well. And of course our defensiveness has engendered stridency and self-righteousness and all the usual sins of the "defended."

But we can call on some pretty strong "bonds of affection."

ID: Yes, I agree completely that along with the vertical relationship with God as basic to communion there is also the horizontal relationship with sisters and brothers in Christ who share in the Trinitarian baptism. There is a larger sense of communion here than only fellowship with Anglican sisters and brothers around the world, for I would want to start the horizontal nature of communion with our ecumenical relationships with other Christians. Here I find the great ecumenical offering of the Episcopal Church and the Anglican Communion in the late nineteenth century known as the Chicago-Lambeth Quadrilateral useful. The Quadrilateral's embrace of Holy Scripture, the two main sacraments of Baptism and Eucharist, the creeds, and the "historic episcopate locally adapted" offers a vision for Christian unity, Christian communion (Appendix 3, #1). Thus I believe communion, "horizontal communion," is all about a shared apostolic faith with all Christians who have gone before us and will come after us. I suspect that here you would say that in the decisions that the Episcopal Church has taken with respect to the place of gay and lesbian people in our church, we have, in fact, abandoned apostolic faith. That is indeed a point I would want to argue with, and we can return to this question when we come to discuss adiaphora next. Can we agree, however, that there is an aspect of the horizontal communion in our shared baptism with all Christians through time and across geographical and cultural boundaries?

Expanding our consideration of the Quadrilateral I would like to suggest that the Windsor Report gives disproportionate attention to the place of Scripture and episcopacy in defining communion while overlooking the sacramental and creedal aspects of communion? It is almost as if we have gone from a Chicago-Lambeth Quadrilateral to a Lambeth Commission "Duolateral."

I find it astonishing, frankly, given the place of liturgy in Anglicanism, that worship, and the Eucharist more specifically, are not lifted up as central defining marks of communion in the Windsor Report. I would argue that Anglicans in particular hold the Book of Common Prayer as helping to identify our common life. While the Book of Common Prayer has been, and continues to be, translated many times in the many different cultural and ecclesial contexts around the Anglican Communion "according to the various exigency of times and occasions," Anglicans the world over find our unity in an ordered liturgical life as annunciated in the Prayer Book. In Anglicanism then, the Book of Common Prayer stands as a common defining gift that undergirds a theological method of *lex orandi lex credendi* (the law of prayer determines the law of belief). The life and witness of the local worshiping community, or parish, where the baptized gather to hear the Word of God proclaimed and the sacraments celebrated, is fundamental to the nature of communion within Anglicanism.

Thus we cannot speak about the horizontal nature of communion without taking into consideration Holy Communion, as in the Lord's Supper, as in the Eucharist. Gathering around the table, together, to be fed with the Body and Blood of Christ is a profound experience of communion. It is around the table that we Anglicans live into an embodied, real, live communion with God and with each other. It is in coming together to be fed of the same bread and wine where the goodwill we have for one another, as well as the anger, hurt, and difficult feelings we harbor against each other, are transformed into "bonds of affection," "bonds of love" for each other. So while you and I, Paul, are "kindly affectioned one to another" (as my bishop Alexander Stewart used to say in his closing blessing at the Eucharist), I dare say that our "bonds of affection" are much deeper than positive experiences shared in Ambridge and Cambridge, or with the Episcopal Church Foundation Fellows Forum. While I deeply appreciate our time together in various meetings of the Episcopal Church, we are linked to each other in a greater Eucharistic Fellowship in such a way that (as Rowan Williams is fond of saying) neither of us can say, "we have no need for the other."

PZ: The same is true of the wider Communion. You and I, Ian, have been given the gift of relationships all over the world, in almost every sector of theological thought and ideology. You have gone to Trinity Episcopal School for Ministry and been welcomed. And I have traveled to Episcopal Divinity School in Cambridge and been welcomed. This pattern has also taken place in our ministries as we have sought to work overseas. My point is, there are some pretty tensile bonds of affection out there, and in here! These can keep us going, and for quite a while.

I do fear that the inability of ECUSA to undertake some collective or formal act of felt regret — let's even say penitence or heartfelt apology for hurt caused and heedless action planned and taken — could stretch those dear bonds to the breaking point. This is what I fear. I actually fear it.

ID: So our bonds of affection are shared with sister and brother Anglicans whether we agree with them or not, and whether they live in Boston or Pittsburgh, in Bombay or Petermaritzburg. Please allow me to share a story here that is an icon for me with respect to the "bonds of affection" that we Anglicans share. Like you I am privileged to serve on one of the four Standing Commissions of the Anglican Communion. While you serve on the Inter-Anglican Theological and Doctrinal Commission (IATDC), I am on the Inter-Anglican Standing Commission on Mission and Evangelism (IASCOME). It was at our IASCOME meeting in December 2003 in Jamaica that (after eight days of working together) the decisions of our General Convention four months earlier finally surfaced. Given that I was the only person from the Episcopal Church in a room with twenty-one other Anglicans from twenty-one other Anglican Churches around the world, it was a pretty difficult place to be. The anger that these sisters and brothers in Christ had towards the Episcopal Church and me (over both the decisions of our General Convention as well as United States military and economic dominance in the world) was palpable. None of us shied away from the fact that our respective churches had said some pretty hurtful things about one another. A few commissioners even had in their possession the statements of impaired communion between the Episcopal Church and their church that their leaders had passed in some form or another. While these statements were indeed significant, we all agreed that in our sharing of the Eucharist each day I should not be excluded from the table nor would others refuse to come to the Lord's Supper if I participated. The love that we had for one other, the love that we celebrated in our common Eucharistic sharing each day, was indeed greater that anything that divided us. I give profound thanks for the sisters and brothers in Christ who hold me and support me in "bonds of affection" (and vice versa) even in the face of the difficulties that our Anglican Communion is experiencing today.

PZ: There are two little things here which I would like to approach. This is in the context of being happy with your response, and especially with the concluding story of your Communion, in the literal sense, with church representatives in the Bahamas. That seems to me to be absolutely right, what happened there. I wish I had been there myself to learn from it and draw comfort from it.

I am a little nervous about your division between Scripture and episcopacy, on the one hand, versus sacraments and creeds, on the other, in reference to points of unity. But notice I say a "little" nervous. I would not wish to elevate any of these four things, save Scripture, to a point of overriding and overruling authority. Not episcopacy, not sacraments as such, and not even creeds, although you will be unsurprised to hear that creeds for me would be important, very important, as they are also to you. And even when I say Scripture, I do not want to make the Bible into a Qur'anic entity, with no distinctions between its parts and its manners of speaking. But generally anyway, I am comfortable with the Bible as chief of all potential authorities.

You seem to be putting a lot of weight on the Communion service, or on the act of receiving Holy Communion, as such, as a point and mode of unity. I think I see where you are coming from. You and I have shared such moments in our ministries, heartfelt moments of unity and intimacy in the context of the Eucharist, which have been powerful and palpable and remembered. But I am wanting to see the Eucharist as more the expression of what is already there — i.e., unity under the lordship of the Crucified Christ. The Eucharist does not, in my experience, create unity so much as express unity.

What I want to think happened in the Bahamas is that the unity under or through the Triune God, of which you spoke, was already there. It was sufficient to override the very strong judgments and antipathies which were in the air. The unity was then most wonderfully expressed, or demonstrated, in the One Bread and the One Cup.

I suspect, too, that a part of what happened was your own humility in being enabled to hear without defensiveness and certainly without counterattack the painful things that must have been said to you, or at least indicated, by fellow Christians there. You allowed, in some way, for yourself to face a certain crucifixion of extreme discomfort. That in itself must have had enormous effect. That at least is a surmise.

ID: Paul, once again your response is most gracious and very much on the mark.

First, a little geographic clarification: our meeting of the Inter-Anglican Standing Commission on Mission and Evangelism was in Jamaica and not the Bahamas. Of course, I would not mind meeting in the Bahamas in December either!

You are quite correct, my experience with the shared Eucharist at the meeting of the Standing Commission did not so much create unity as express the unity that we had in the Triune God. The unity in the Triune God "was sufficient to override the very strong judgments and antipathies which were in the air." And, boy, were those feelings there in Jamaica. You surmised correctly that I had to sit and listen without defensiveness and without attack about how actions of the Episcopal Church and the United States on many levels have caused hurt and pain around the world. I cannot say it was an enjoyable experience but one that I am thankful, by the grace of God, I was able to have. Deep listening and sharing across difficult issues in the unity of the Triune God is exactly what I think communion is all about. So the unity, the communion, that we live in the Inter-Anglican Standing Commission on Mission and Evangelism was indeed most wonderfully expressed, or demonstrated, in the One Bread and the One Cup.

PZ: Ian, the only other thing I want to say is that we do well, you and I, to stay with our high doctrine of the Holy Spirit in all this discussion. Which is to say, I am delighted to affirm the impulse and driving character of the Spirit as being prior and over and more important to the life of the church than episcopacy, sacraments, and even creeds. For me, the Spirit speaks powerfully and normally through the Word of God, the Scriptures. But I am willing also, with you, to give him a little wiggle room in other sectors! That was sort of a jest, but you know what I mean. Let's invite the Holy Spirit of Christ as a sort of Aslan figure into all these batterings by and in the church and our own beleaguered spirits. That is a very good place — or rather, He/She is a very good place — to end, and begin.

ID: I am also in agreement that having a high doctrine of the Holy Spirit helps in these matters. For it is by the Spirit that we live and move and have our being. How I wish that there was as high of an embrace of the Holy Spirit in the Windsor Report. For me, life in Spirit means that the securities and certainties of my closely held positions are most wonderfully upset by the provisionality and newness that the Holy Spirit continues to bring into being. Thanks be to God.

What is the report's take on authority? Autonomy? Adiaphora? Subsidiarity?

PZ: The report is fairly predictable on all these areas. Again, if it had not ducked the *big* issue, which is the theology, pro and con, of the decision to ordain an actively homosexual bishop and bless same-sex unions, all these "takes" on big issues would have been more useful than they are.

   The report puts the Bible squarely in the middle of our concept of authority. As I have already said, too much is made of the untransparency of Scripture, its being subject to several interpretive grids. I do not accept that. In any event, authority, or rather the lip service of authority, is given to the Bible. Also, bishops are regarded as public teachers, not just icons or symbols of organic unity. That emphasis on bishops as teachers is much to the good. But it all breaks down because the big question of human sexuality itself, which is absolutely clear-cut from the standpoint of the text of the Bible, is ruled out of court. (How come this evasion has not been more vividly lanced in the media and in public I do not understand. It seems Swiftian to me.)

ID: We have talked quite a bit about the nature of authority described in the Windsor Report. I think we are basically in agreement that the report is quite good on the nature of biblical authority. We share some concern as to the nature of episcopal authority put forward in the report in that it all too easily slides into centralization around a monarchical presentation of the bishop. I do not believe that you and I are against bishops, or even the authority that bishops have in Anglicanism. Rather (as good United States citizens who believe in the power of democracy) you and I stand squarely on the shoulders of William White, who argued for bishops by ballot with a key role for the laity in deciding such. Episcopal authority is just fine as long as it is shared with all the people of God, including the laity!

I have noted above that I think the Windsor Report neglects to consider the creeds as a locus of authority in Anglicanism. Our mutual friend Professor Bob Hughes, Professor of Theology at the seminary of the University of the South in Sewanee, Tennessee, in a presentation he made in Nashville just after the Windsor Report was released, was very eloquent on this point. Bob, the good patristic theologian that he is, stresses that for the church fathers, and their successors, the Nicene Creed is the church's final statement of what is absolutely essential in the rule of faith for all believers. The Windsor Report's emphasis on scriptural and episcopal authority while neglecting creedal authority is thus a significant omission. Bob says it best: "In sum, the report, by going directly from scripture to episcopate, produces a picture of the bishop as a kind of Lone Ranger bible teacher, removed from any of the three restraints that form the essence of communion: union of the apostolic office not only with the biblical twelve, but also with the '318 holy fathers' of the first Council of Nicea and the entire conciliar tradition as embodied in the creeds. It tends to separate the authority of individual bishops, especially primates, from the conciliar collegiality with their peers in the present and cuts off the entire office from its proper context within the baptismal covenant community and Eucharistic Assembly. It is almost as if scripture is viewed as giving individual bishops a kind of authority *in propria persona,* a concept that violates all the principles of the Reformation, let alone of the American experiment with democratization." To this I would say, "Amen, Bob."

Laying aside the discussion of autonomy for a moment, I want to look at adiaphora next, especially since it links so close with this discussion of the creeds. "Adiaphora" is defined as "things which do not make a difference, matters regarded as nonessential, issues about which one can disagree without dividing the Church" (par. 87). Now if we see "the Nicene Creed as the sufficient statement of the Christian faith" (Appendix 3, #1) then it could be argued that any other things not taken up by the creed are adiaphora. This, I think, is a simplistic either/or with which I am not comfortable. Once again, I find Bob Hughes's Nashville presentation helpful here. Bob points out that while the Nicene Creed defines matters that are essential to the faith, there are different levels of meaning for other nonessential matters of church life. Bob emphasizes that there are matters which are important (such as all ethical questions) and hence not adiaphora, but at the same time these matters are *not essential* for salvation in that they do not touch on creedal faith. While adiaphora could be taken as constituting only things that are "indifferent," of little or no significance to the Christian life, there remain many aspects of the Christian faith that are thus greater than adiaphora but not creedally essential. Too many sisters and brothers in Christ through the generations and even today have died over aspects of the faith that are not mentioned in the Nicene Creed for me to reduce all noncreedal questions to adiaphora (par. 93). The problem, however, is that what is of the higher order while not being creedally essential in one time or place can be adiaphora in another context and vice versa. This, of course, leads to the key question: who gets to decide what is adiaphora or not (par. 95).

PZ: I like the report's attention to the idea of adiaphora. We are all aware of a hundred and even a thousand points of church life that can differ from place to place yet still be regarded as part of a thoroughly authentic Christian culture and praxis. Thus I can attend a High Mass in the Diocese of Albany and recognize myself, as it were, thoroughly in the worship and focus of the service. Or, I can attend a "lower" renewal service on James Island, South Carolina, and be utterly addressed and helped. And the many instances of adiaphora go way beyond the ceremonial.

We all wish to give a lot of leeway to local custom and practice. But what has happened in New Hampshire and in New Westminster is not adiaphora. The application will not stick. I see these developments as an overturning of the inspired Christian anthropology of Original inherited sin and the dramatic Christology of Christ's death on the Cross for the sin of the world. I am convinced that these recent developments are a test-tube expression of the phenomenon that is really rightly called "cheap grace." I conceive of these innovations as the piggy-backing by large sectors of the Episcopal Church on to American ideas of "choice" and "autonomy" (in a brash and lovingless mode) that underwrote the unilateral war against Iraq. These are not adiaphora. They are invasive symptoms of "another religion," which is an odd marriage of USA-style Pelagianism with the over-riding hunger of a passionate constituency to receive a christening for what most Christians will never not regard as a species of self-damaging evangelistic narcissism.

ID: As the Windsor Report appropriately points out, the question of who gets to decide is also linked to the concept of subsidiarity. The report is clear on what it means by subsidiarity, namely, "the principle that matters in the Church should be decided as close to the local level as possible" (par. 94). Now all of this sounds quite good, especially to my American Episcopalian democratic ears. But my hermeneutics of suspicion forces me to ask the question: Where did this emphasis on subsidiarity come from, in Anglicanism and in the wider church? Whose end does subsidiarity serve? To the best of my knowledge the application of subsidiarity to describe Anglican polity first arose in the "Virginia Report," the 1998 report of the Inter-Anglican Theological and Doctrinal

Commission. In the Virginia Report, subsidiarity was hallowed as an appropriate description of how we Anglicans go about our decision making. The principle that matters in the church should be decided as close to the local level as possible sounds like good Anglican polity until we discover that the concept of subsidiarity was first introduced by Pope Pius XI in his 1931 encyclical *Quadragesimo Anno*. My Roman Catholic colleagues who are social ethicists all agree that Pius XI used subsidiarity to get him off of the hook of having to deal with emerging fascism in Europe in the first half of the twentieth century. As long as the Pope defined fascism as a matter of local concern to the church in Germany or Italy, then he did not have to take a stand against the horrors being perpetrated by Hitler or Mussolini. So in the first case, some can use subsidiarity to avoid asking themselves difficult questions. In the second case, any discussion of subsidiarity must ask: from which direction does the power come, from the bottom up (as we Anglicans would like to believe) or from the top to the bottom (as in the case of Pope Pius XI)? Knowing the etiology of subsidiarity in the 1931 encyclical, I would be more comfortable not using the term at all to describe Anglican polity.

PZ: "Subsidiarity" is just a subset of the "adiaphora" idea. Subsidiarity is the idea that church problems should be decided "on the ground," or thoroughly in context. This is related to the idea of "contextualization," of which theologians of liberation have made so much. And yes, surely it is true that "context" trumps carpetbaggers! Who wants a "furriner" coming in and telling you what to do, when you have to live here? The church on the ground requires protection against "outside agitators," as such persons were once known during the civil rights movement in the American South. Yet isn't it ironic? The "outside agitators" were pretty much right. In cases of extreme and consistent violations of human rights, it seemed to take outsiders to bring a different look and create change. Interestingly, I think the principle of subsidiarity breaks down in the case of ECUSA. We *need* "outside agitators" (like the jurisdiction-crossing African Primates) to help us come to our senses! This is how I really feel. By virtue of our conscious heedlessness, ECUSA has no claim on subsidiarity, in this particular case of heresy in faith and morals. We require the presence of "outside agitators."

The report understands provincial autonomy to be an important feature of Anglicanism. Here again, in principle, I have no problem. Each local church, over an obvious geographical entity, should have the right to determine its own affairs as it sees fit, *unless* its determination touches a vital nerve of catholic faith and practice. Such nerves are not subject to a particular province's believing that its "autonomy" extends to the life's blood of the religion. ECUSA used its legal "autonomy" to go beyond what is catholic and evangelical and mainstream. Thus it went beyond what is allowed by the concept itself.

ID: While I want to nuance the Windsor Report's discussion of adiaphora and subsidiarity, I do want to embrace the report's take on autonomy. I agree that the diversity at the heart of the Anglican Communion is "enshrined in the autonomy of individual provinces" (par. 72). The report's historical review of the development of autonomy in the Anglican Communion is well done (par. 74–75). I find great sympathy with the report's main point that autonomy "is not the same thing as sovereignty or independence." Rather autonomy "more closely resembles the orthodox polity of 'autocephaly,' which denotes autonomy in communion" (par. 75). The key here is that autonomy only makes sense if the autonomous body is in relationship with another autonomous body. There is no unrelated autonomy. I think quoting the report here is very worthwhile because I find here one of the best expositions of the nature of communion in the whole report. "A body is thus, in this sense, 'autonomous' only in relation to others; autonomy exists in relation with a wider community or system of which the autonomous entity forms a part. The word 'autonomous' in this sense actually implies not an isolated individualism, but the idea of being free to determine one's own life within a wider obligation to others. The key idea is autonomy-in-communion, that is, freedom held within interdependence. The autonomy of each Anglican province therefore implies that the church lives in relation to, and exercises its autonomy most fully in the context of the global Communion" (par. 76). I'm afraid that this kind of interrelatedness, this kind of identity in relation to others, is not something that Americans do well. While we as a nation are great innovators, great respecters of the rights of the individual, we are not so great on living lives of mutuality and interdependence. Our country's most recent incursion into Iraq is a case in point. So I think there is much in this definition of "autonomy in relationship" from which we Americans, particularly we American Anglicans, can learn. I believe that if we had deeply nurtured relationships in mission with our sister and brother Anglicans around the world over the last few decades, the Anglican Communion would not be in such a difficult place today.

PZ: Ian, you have, quite effectively and even brilliantly, sidestepped what I wrote in order to present a solid argument concerning both creedal "weightings" of issues in theology, and also subsidiarity in relation to the concept of authority. You did here what successful public figures do with media interviews: you stuck to your line and refused to be detoured from it.

I admire you! And won't complain.

I also had a revealing little experience while reading what you have written. I started in medias res and thought somehow I was still reading my own stuff. In fact, because I admire Bob Hughes as much as you and had been taken with his address concerning important Christian issues that are *not* covered in the creeds, I thought I must have somehow forgotten what I had written. I also sinfully began to say to myself, Gosh, I really sound like I know what I'm talking about!

Then I got to the part about the papal encyclical of 1931 and realized: It's Ian! I'm thinking Ian's words are my own.

Now unlike Marvin Gaye, I didn't immediately say, "Ain't that peculiar." Rather, I thought, we must really be getting under each other's skin now. So, hooray!

ID: Paul, I must admit that I too am delighting in the fact that we are "getting under each other's skins." It's rather amazing that two individuals, who many in the church would be quick to put at odds with each other, are in fact learning to live and love each other in new ways through the processes of discussion, conversation, and listening. So I thank God for that, and I thank God for you and our little conversation on the Windsor Report.

You are correct that in my response to the question, I stayed on message, or more specifically stayed on my message. I have had enough experience with the media to know that the best defense is a good offense (Vince Lombardi, I think). So right you are on calling me on that.

PZ: Just two final words then: Your sentence, "There is no unrelated autonomy," is a fine one. Autonomy is a fine thing, yes; but autonomy without relationship is spite and sin.

Also your repeated phrase, "autonomy-in-communion," strikes just the right note. It strikes the right note Reformationally and also biblically. God enables us to be truly free, even autonomous in the Kantian and Enlightenment sense. But this freedom is always in the context of love, which is what you and I are naming the "bonds of affection." So I am right alongside you in what you have said concerning autonomy and solidarity.

Hey, and we'll get back to "my" issues another time.... (I can live with that.)

ID: I wish that the idea of "autonomy in relationship" or "communion in relationship" was mine, but it isn't. It comes from the Windsor Report itself (par. 72–86). The presentation of the relational nature of autonomy I find to be one of the most important offerings of the report and one I would like to see lifted up in our and other discussions. I do appreciate your own addition that "autonomy without relationship is spite and sin." I've seen quite a bit of this kind of spite and sin across the Anglican Communion as of late. When one province or church in the Anglican Communion functions as if it is not aware of or in direct relationship with another church or province, or when one part of the Anglican Communion declares it is in impaired communion with another church or province, there I find spite and sin. So I am in agreement with the Archbishop of Canterbury in his Epiphany letter to the primates when he said we all need to repent of such sin and spite. As Archbishop Williams wrote: "To repent before one another is to see that we have failed in our witness as God's new community, failed to live in the full interdependence of love...."

Where did the "Four Instruments of Unity" come from? Why Is there an emphasis on such?

PZ: The emergence of the "Four Instruments of Unity" reflects an important historical phenomenon: the consistent and long-term weakening of the old and more ancient instruments of unity which were enshrined by the Articles, the Homilies, and the Prayer Book. Before the more "liberal" tilt of English and American Anglicanism, not to mention South African Anglicanism, which began in the later 1800s, it was enough to say that Anglican authority lay in the theology of the Thirty-Nine Articles of Religion (1561), to which every rector had to swear essential agreement; the Homilies, or statutory sermons originating from the Reformation settlement under Queen Elizabeth I; and the Book of Common Prayer, which, despite some minor alteration and additions over the years, was essentially derived from the orthodox and Protestant Prayer Book of 1552, made more or less binding for three centuries in the Prayer Book of 1662. These instruments — the Articles, the Homilies, and the Prayer Book — were all that was required to say one was an Anglican.

ID: Over the last thirty-five years there has been an increasing emphasis on, and proliferation of, structures and "instruments of unity" at the global Anglican Communion level. I am not so much in agreement with you, Paul, that this "instrumentalist" approach to unity has risen because of "the consistent and long-term weakening of the old and more ancient instruments of unity which were enshrined in the Articles, the Homilies, and the Prayer

Book." Rather, I believe that the increasingly multicultural and pluralistic nature of the Anglican Communion as it has grown outside of the West in the last half of the twentieth century has caused a profound crisis as to issues of identity and authority in the Anglican Communion. The cultural hegemony of the Anglo-American alliance of the Church of England and the Episcopal Church has begun to crack in Anglicanism, and anthems by Titcomb and Tallis sung by boy choirs in Oxford or in New York City can no longer hold us together. As a result in the last decade and a half, in particular, many have looked to inter-Anglican structures as possible agents of authority with the power to clarify issues of Anglican identity, using juridical means if necessary. These structural responses to the challenges of identity in an increasingly diverse and plural Anglican Communion, although well meaning, might not best serve the Communion at this time.

The articulation of structures or instruments of unity in response to questions of identity and authority in the Anglican Communion has been part of inter-Anglican discussions at least since the mid-1980s. At the 1987 meeting of the Anglican Consultative Council (ACC) in Singapore, a discussion paper was presented on "Unity in Diversity within the Anglican Communion." This paper, drafted by a small working group under the Chairmanship of the Most Rev. Robin Eames, Archbishop of Armagh (and also the Chair of the Lambeth Commission that produced the Windsor Report), noted "four traditional instruments for maintaining the unity in diversity of the Anglican Communion," namely, the Archbishop of Canterbury, Lambeth Conferences, the Anglican Consultative Council, and the Primates Meetings.

PZ: Whenever the substantial and material constitutives of unity become eroded or questioned over time, the argument always pitches over to more superficial things, such as canons, rules, hierarchs, process, and other horizontal entities. This is what has happened in Anglicanism. If confidence in the Bible's verbal authority is weakened, if the very evangelical and Reformational theology of the Articles is questioned, if thus the Homilies begin to sound, in their sixteenth-century formulations and style, like Martian, and if the Prayer Book itself is substantially altered and updated in content from context to context: well, then, some more "visual" or "legal" yardsticks have to be researched in order to provide for unity.

This, in my opinion, is where the "Four Instruments of Unity" are derived. (And note that now even a *fifth*, the so-called Covenant, has been added by the report putatively.) The Archbishop of Canterbury is not sufficient to guarantee any deep and material unity among Christians, save as a historic and to some extent romantic symbol. The Lambeth Conference, a very recent thing in real terms, is also a collegial but not legislative body. ECUSA's contempt for what the Lambeth Conference determined in 1998 concerning homosexuality reflects the inadequacy of that Conference as an effective external instrument of unity. The Anglican Consultative Council is a body with which most Anglicans are entirely unfamiliar in reality and practice. And the primates? Well, that sounds a little better. The primates could function as a sort of "upper house" of the Anglican Communion legislatively. But can they? Will they? Thus far they have not functioned that way. Although it is fully true to say that "traditionalists" are all and have all been hoping that the primates will function this way when they meet in February of 2005.

The second question is now easily answered. Why is there now such an emphasis on these "Four Instruments of Unity"? It is because the old instruments, which are deeper, richer, and more profound, have lost the confidence of an influential section of First-World Anglican leaders. These people no longer regard the penitential and atonement-focused spirituality and content of the Articles, Homilies, and Prayer Book as apt and sufficient to the needs of contemporary people. The problem is theological. The contemporary stress on horizontal forms of unity like the ACC and so on reflects the sad turning away from vertical measures of unity such as the inspired Elizabethan Articles of a confessional Anglican faith.

ID: While the Four Instruments of Unity gained increasing notice
in the late 1980s and 1990s as representing the polity of the
Anglican Communion, the instruments were given even greater
significance with the publication of the Virginia Report by the
Inter-Anglican Theological and Doctrinal Commission (IATDC)
just before the 1998 Lambeth Conference, as I noted above. The
report was offered by IATDC as a means of identifying the nature of communion in Anglicanism. The concluding chapter of the
report, in particular, presents the fullest exposition of the Four Instruments of Unity. Its final reflections underscore the importance
of "structures" and "instruments" for effecting communion at the
global level. There is so much overlap between the recommendations of the Virginia Report and the Windsor Report as to place
of the Four Instruments of Unity in the Anglican Communion
that I am tempted to call the Windsor Report the Virginia Report
Redux.

At the 1998 Lambeth Conference the Virginia Report was not
so much a matter of discussion and debate but rather a backdrop
for all discussions related to inter-Anglican unity. The bishops
gathering in Canterbury for the conference were presented with
the report as a summary statement of the work of the Theological
and Doctrinal Commission. Perhaps the planners of the conference hoped that the findings of IATDC presented in the Virginia
Report could help the global gathering of episcopal leaders find
their way forward through what would become quite contentious
discussions and debates, particularly as the bishops considered
matters dealing with human sexuality.

While the Virginia Report itself was not debated at the Lambeth Conference of 1998, resolutions were drawn up and passed
by the conference that built on the work of IATDC. Resolution
III.8 on the Virginia Report commended the report and requested
"the Primates to initiate and monitor a decade of study in each
province on the report and, in particular on *'whether effective
communion, at all levels, does not require appropriate instruments, with due safeguards, not only for legislation, but also for
oversight.'* " The specific bolstering of the instruments was taken

up in Resolution III.6: on "Instruments of the Anglican Communion." Resolution III.6 advanced the role of primates seeking to make them the episcopal members of the Anglican Consultative Council and also asking "the Primates Meeting, under the Presidency of the Archbishop of Canterbury, (to) include among its responsibilities... intervention in cases of exceptional emergency which are incapable of internal resolution within provinces and giving of guidelines on the limits of Anglican diversity...." Finally, Resolution III.6 recommended that the bishops representing each province in the Anglican Consultative Council should be the primates of the province, thus excluding other episcopal representation in the only international, representative council of the Church. Whether deliberately intended or not, the instruments of unity have been advanced as structures that bind the Anglican Communion together, and the Primates Meeting, in particular, is increasingly perceived as a locus of authority for the global Communion that is able to arbitrate disputes within Anglicanism.

We might recall that the Primates Meeting itself grew out of a move to contain the movement for the ordination of women in the late 1970s. Sir Paul Reeves recalled for me during his tenure as Anglican Observer to the United Nations that when he was Archbishop of Aotearoa, New Zealand, and Polynesia, he attended the first informal meeting of primates called by Presiding Bishop of the Episcopal Church John M. Allin, which took in Washington, D.C., shortly after the 1976 General Convention authorized the ordination of women. It was the Lambeth Conference of 1978 that then recommended a regular meeting of the primates of the Anglican Communion on an every-other-year basis. This biannual meeting was made a yearly meeting at the Primates Meeting in Oporto, Portugal, in 2000. So I think we need to be a little careful as to how we read the history of the development of the Primates Meeting as an "Instrument of Unity." While the Windsor Report celebrates the effective functioning of the Instruments with respect to the acceptance of women's ordination (par. 15), I think it can equally be argued that the process of reception of the ordination of women has not been as merry and straightforward as presented in the report. The history of women's ordination in

the Windsor Report significantly overlooks the hurt that women
and their male supporters have received in the movement to ordain women across the Anglican Communion. And the process
of reception of women's ordination, particularly in episcopal orders, is far from over in the Anglican Communion, with levels of
impaired communion existing today between Anglican churches,
some of which recognize women's ordination and some of which
do not.

Finally, in all of this discussion on the Four Instruments it is important to note that at the meeting of the Anglican Consultative
Council in Dundee, Scotland, in 1999, the resolutions of the 1998
Lambeth Conference growing out of the Virginia Report were
summarily turned down. Our own General Convention in 2000,
in Resolution C009, turned away from the findings of the Virginia
Report and encouraged "the continuing evolution of conciliar
modes of discernment in the practice of an authority." Further,
I would argue that the Virginia Report has not been enthusiasti-
cally received across the Communion since its release in 1998. Yet
here in the Windsor Report we have many of the recommendations of the Virginia Report coming to the forefront once again.
In "Appendix One: Reflections on the Instruments of Unity," not
only is the 1998 recommendation to have the primates sit as the
episcopal representatives on the Anglican Consultative Council
brought back (Appendix 1, #1) but the Commission recommends
that the Standing Committee of the Primates Meeting become
ex officio members of the ACC and of the ACC Standing Committee, thus making them trustees of the Anglican Communion
(Appendix 1, #2). Further, Appendix 1 seeks to strengthen some
Lambeth Conference Resolutions to become "definitive teaching
of the Anglican Communion" and suggests that the "Primates
Meeting should serve formally as the Standing Committee of the
Lambeth Conference and as such should monitor developments in
furtherance of resolutions of the Lambeth Conference in addition
to the process of reception" (Appendix 1, #4 and #5).

I do not know about you, Paul, but the centralization of power
and authority in the "Four Instruments of Unity," particularly in
the Primates Meeting, as we have seen over the last two decades,

seems very un-Anglican to me. Maybe it is the blood of my Presbyterian grandfather from Scotland flowing through my veins, but I am very leery of this ecclesiological slide toward Rome that I find in both the Virginia Report and the Windsor Report.

PZ: I'm *glad* you got carried away!

Ian, there is a consistent theme coming through our conversation. It is sounding loud and clear! It is the theme of centralization versus dispersed authority, or, to put it more colloquially, it is the theme of control versus freedom.

ID: Paul, yes, I believe that there is a common theme in our discussion and that is the "theme of centralization versus dispersed authority, or, to put it more colloquially, it is the theme of control versus freedom." And I think we are in agreement that there is a profound identity crisis in the Anglican Communion that exacerbates these discussions over centralization versus dispersed authority, control versus freedom. In so many discussions of the Windsor Report, on the right and on the left, I have seldom seen these themes raised. Rather, one side or the other is too busy trying to posit a position on "moratorium this" or "moratorium that" rather than stepping back and looking at the larger, more substantive themes in the report. So I hope our conversation is of service here.

PZ: What you have done first here is to root the "turn" to centralization in our church not in a theological loss of faith, but rather in the diversity of the worldwide Anglican family. You are saying that the push to work through so-called instruments of unity is derived from an identity crisis. We don't know who we are. I won't give up beating the drum on the loss of theological nerve — which I think is true of ECUSA as a whole. But I admit the empirical fact that the worldwide character of Anglicanism in a contentious and divided world forces us to confront issues of identity. We have no choice.

Yet you and I are continuing to sound the same note: that the resolution to our problems does not consist in a reassertion of hierarchy. That smacks of panic. That smacks of fear. And it certainly does not enable moral autonomy in the proper sense of the term.

Again, as I cannot really tire of saying, the Bible, as a whole, should provide the Christian Church with a reasonable and mostly self-interpreting charter. The Bible should be able to offer the church a mandate and a checkpoint. I do not mean a Qur'anic checkpoint, or what people often say is a "fundamentalist" checkpoint, or even a wholly verbal and declaratory checkpoint. But the Bible as a whole provides guidance and authority for most questions of religion and ethics. I would even say that it provides authority for all the deep and presenting issues of our relationship to God, and also to one another.

Are we talking a "paper pope"? I do not think so. This is why, for example, Bible-believing Christians can differ legitimately concerning the ordination of women to the priesthood. That is to say, you can read both a no and a yes to such a question from out of the Scriptures. Scripture does not offer an absolutely clear signal on that one.

But on the current presenting symptom, Scripture does speak without a forked tongue. Scripture does go up just one road on the presenting question of the day. And I am comfortable with letting that stand, letting that be more powerful and compelling, not to mention constraining, than any derived "instruments of unity."

When we try to write our next book together, O conversation partner, I suggest we look at the Holy Spirit. I suspect that the doctrine of the Holy Spirit, and the forms in which the Holy Spirit speaks to humans and the church, is the heart of our future discussion. This is a discussion I would also like to have, quite seriously, with Gene Robinson, as well. I, like you, am just too Protestant to accept a humanly derived instrument of unity. Unlike you, perhaps, I am willing to ascribe to the Bible a divine origin, in the overwhelming main. But we really need one day, you and I, to look systematically at the work of the Holy Spirit in the now.

ID: I'm also in agreement with you that our identity lies in the Holy Scripture. As you say "the Bible, as a whole, should provide the Christian Church with a reasonable and mostly self-interpreting charter." I do not see you as using the Bible, as you say, as a Qur'anic checkpoint. Like I said, I would never call you a "fundamentalist." Instead, I agree with you that "the Bible as a whole provides guidance and authority for most questions of religion and ethics." The operative phase here is "as a whole," because any verse or set of verses in the Bible can be misused to proof text a particular position while losing the larger story, the metanarrative if you will, of God's love for all creation. See, I told you I was not a card-carrying postmodernist, or else I could not affirm the truth of the metanarrative of God in the Bible. To that end, I am willing (contrary to what you might think) to ascribe to the Bible a divine origin. And I have publicly sworn in my ordination vows that "I believe the Holy Scriptures of the Old and New Testaments to be the Word of God, and to contain all things necessary to salvation."

    I like the idea of our next conversation/book being on the Holy Spirit. But I would gladly give my conversation place to the Bishop of New Hampshire. My guess is that he could say a whole lot about how the Holy Spirit has worked in his life. Wouldn't it be great if the Bishop of New Hampshire and the Bishop of Pittsburgh could have the conversation instead of you and me? That would go a long way towards modeling the nature of communion in relationship for the church and for the world.

What is the relationship between canon law and covenant? How are these reconciled with the Four Instruments of Unity?

PZ: To begin with, any sort of "reliance" upon canon law in the Anglican Communion generally, especially in the interests of enforcing discipline or uniformity, is a very new thing. The report observes this practically "implicit" character of canon law in our tradition, rather than its explicit operation and use. It has really never normally been an issue. It has not been an issue in seeking to "bring to heel" a recalcitrant Province. Yes, there have been bishops out of order theologically, such as Colenso in Natal and, in my view, Richard Holloway in Scotland and John Spong over here. And even then, in these fairly extreme cases, canon law has rarely been invoked. Canon law has certainly never succeeded in silencing one of these "troublers of Israel." I'm not sure I can think of a single case where it has worked in this kind of situation.

But now — and it is a sign of the times — canon law is more and more mentioned. Certainly the Eames Commission was feared at times to be "in the hands of the lawyers." This would have made its approach to law quite well in harmony with the ruling American mind-set. Let the judges decide! Let the judicial branch decide! Let controversy all come down to points of law. Jarndyce vs. Jarndyce in the church, as well as in the world generally. Ian, I resist this way of thinking. And I think I see its obtrusion into the Windsor Report.

ID: Paul, I agree with you completely that the etiology of turning to canon law and/or covenant in inter-Anglican affairs arises from "interests of enforcing discipline or uniformity" across Anglicanism. I further agree with you that such a response to differences in Anglicanism is a very new thing for Anglicans worldwide. As is becoming my custom in this conversation, I think it is worthwhile to do a little institutional history here to see where these conversations about canon law in the Anglican Communion have been fostered.

The first time that canon law was seriously engaged as a means for fostering communion in Anglicanism was at the Primates Meeting in March 2001 at Kanuga Conference Center in North Carolina. It was at the 2001 Primates Meeting that Professor Norman Doe, director of the Centre for Law and Religion, at Cardiff University in Wales, presented a paper on "Canon Law and Communion." It is important to note here that the same Professor Doe was a key member of the Lambeth Commission that produced the Windsor Report. In his 2001 paper to the primates, Professor Doe put forward the idea that the canon law of each church in the Anglican Communion could be more fully developed to enhance communion across Anglicanism globally. He suggested: "A Declaration of Common Anglican Canon Law and Polity could be issued by the Primates Meeting, in the form of a concordat; all primates would be signatories. The statement would not of itself be law, issuing from the global moral order, but rather would set out the programme for canonical revision in each church." Professor Doe's paper did not argue that the Primates Meeting should have increased authority for determining or arbitrating communion, but rather the primates could play a key role in helping each Anglican church to develop canon law themselves that would lead to greater unity in the Communion.

The same idea was raised again by Professor Doe in the paper he, himself, produced for the Lambeth Commission called "Communion and Autonomy in Anglicanism: Nature and Maintenance." In this incredibly well-researched and well-documented paper of 45 pages and 452 footnotes, Professor Doe significantly advances many of his ideas first put forward in 2001. Basic to both papers was the need to develop a *ius communionis* (communion law) within each Anglican church in the Anglican Communion. In the words of Professor Doe, such communion law is "a body of law which might be created by each church to translate global conventions about communion into a meaningful and binding reality for each church, and to enable that church to be responsible for its own maintenance of communion with other Anglican churches in an exercise of autonomy by that church. In short, for each church to develop, perhaps under the guidance of the Primates Meeting, its own *ius communionis*."

PZ: Anyway, covenant is just a making-more-forceful of the judicial principle in Anglicanism. It is a way to spell out what has heretofore been unsaid but accepted: that no one provincial member of the Communion family will jump out in front, ahead of the line generally. Covenant is just a written form of what has always been unwritten, a proper "gentleman's agreement," rooted in these famous bonds of affection, namely, that consultation and cooperation, even Grace in relationship, will win over one-sidedness and caprice. So I have no problem with the covenant proposed by the Commission, although it is an admission of defeat from the standpoint of the old way.

How to reconcile the covenant concept with the Four Instruments of Unity? Well, the concept is just an addition. It makes Five in place of Four. And given the American reluctance to admit fault here, we could end up with six, or seven, or maybe eight one day. The Four Instruments should have worked in this case. The Archbishop spoke, very clearly, before the consecration of Gene Robinson. Lambeth had already spoken, very clearly and also overwhelmingly. The ACC had supported Lambeth. The primates sure had. None of these "Instruments" proved up to the enforcement task. Will a covenant be sufficient? Highly doubtful. The Presiding Bishop has already proposed a lengthy, questioning, options-open study of the covenant idea. This he said in the letter he wrote from London just after the report was published. And even if we get it, if we get the covenant in ECUSA, do you honestly think it will prevail where the other Four Instruments failed and were disregarded so crashingly? *J'espère que oui, mais je le doute.*

ID: I must admit, having read both of these papers previous to the release of the Windsor Report (both were available on the Anglican Communion Web site), that I was surprised to see that the idea for a communion law for each church became somewhat abbreviated and a new "Anglican Covenant" suggestion was added to the original idea. Specifically, the Commission suggests that "a brief law (that each Anglican church would subscribe to) would be preferable to and more feasible than incorporation by each church of an elaborate and all-embracing canon defining inter-Anglican relations" (par. 117). Such a brief "communion law" in each Anglican church "might authorize its primate (or equivalent) to sign (a) Covenant on behalf of that church and commit the church to adhere to the terms of the Covenant" (par. 118). The Covenant, in turn, "would make explicit and forceful the loyalty of bonds of affection which govern the relationships between the churches of

the Communion. The Covenant could deal with: The acknowl-
edgement of common identity, the relationships of communion;
the commitments of communion; the exercise of autonomy in
communion; and the management of communion affairs (including disputes)" (par. 118). A suggested draft covenant is found in
Appendix 2 of the Windsor Report. It is important to note that
this draft is simply offered as an example of what such a covenant might include. Because of the crush of time to produce their
report, the Lambeth Commission did not consider as a whole in
their meetings what was offered in Appendix 2. Rather they empowered one of their own to produce the draft in time for the
publication of the Windsor Report.

Now in theory I am not against the idea of an Anglican
Communion Covenant that each Anglican church might embrace
through *their own polity processes*. I must admit that I like the
idea of a communion covenant over communion law. To me,
covenants are fundamentally about relationships to which one
gives oneself voluntarily, while laws can be seen as body of gov-
erning principles under which one is forced to live. Covenants
are freewill voluntary offerings from one to another, while laws
are binding entities whose locus of authority is external to oneself. As Anglican churches, we have a tradition of covenants that
help to clarify our relationships with other ecumenical churches,
such as the Porvoo agreement between the Church of England
and the Baltic Lutheran churches, and Called to Common Mission between the Episcopal Church and the Evangelical Lutheran
Church in America. So I am in agreement with the Archbishop of
Canterbury when he said in his Advent 2004 letter to the primates
of the Anglican Communion, "We have experience of making
covenants with our ecumenical partners; why should there not
be appropriate commitments which we can freely and honestly
make with one another?"

While I am theoretically open to the idea of an Anglican Cove-
nant, I am decidedly against the process suggested by the Windsor
Report that gives blanket authority to the primate or the Presiding
Bishop of the Episcopal Church to enter into such a Covenant.

Other churches in the Anglican Communion might give their primates such authority, but that is clearly not our polity. Only the General Convention, the highest legislative body of the Episcopal Church, can enter into covenants on behalf of our church. Once again, I'm afraid the Windsor Report is giving too much authority to the primates to arbitrate Anglican Communion affairs.

Finally, I am in agreement with you that the Windsor Report seems to suggest that an Anglican Covenant might be considered as a possible fifth instrument of unity. To me this is more a marriage of convenience rather than a well-thought-out plan. Somehow the Lambeth Commission's two discussions about how to adjudicate communion, namely, the instrumentalist (Four Instruments of Unity) and canonical (Anglican Covenant), needed to be reconciled, and suggesting that the covenant might function as a instrument of unity was offered as a plausible suggestion. As I have alluded to already in this conversation, I do not believe that either instruments or covenants can in and of themselves bring about communion within Anglicanism. Rather communion is a gift from God that we live into as we join with sisters and brothers in Christ in service to God's reconciling and restoring mission in the world.

PZ: *Bestimmt!* We are absolutely agreed, Ian. What I like especially about what you have said here is your providing the timeline and the actual background facts to the reliance of the Windsor Report on the "covenant" ideas of Sir Norman Doe. You then show its weakness, in that our ECUSA polity is General Convention–based rather than primate-based, such that the Presiding Bishop cannot speak for us in relation to such a "covenant." You also demonstrate the fact that such "canon law" thinking in this international context is very new to Anglicanism. You finally regard the "covenant" as a potential fifth instrument of unity. And why should we stop at five? It all indicates an identity crisis to which principles of law are never, Christianly speaking, the proper resolution. Grace alone resolves conflict of this depth. And may I quote Burt Bacharach and Tonio Kroger: "Love's (still) the answer"?! Which is to say, consideration and "space" and wide latitude: these are the ultimate "instruments of unity" in the proleptic Kingdom of God.

ID: Thanks, Paul. Now, I know that not everyone is enamored with institutional history as I am. I think it is important, however, that we take the time to look at the origins of many of the ideas and suggestions raised in the Windsor Report. All too often we in the church go merrily on our way with the recommendations of one report or another, while neglecting to do the research necessarily to cite the preexisting conversations. This is often to our loss and detriment. For without knowing where items came from, we cannot appropriately evaluate the question at hand with adequate knowledge and insight.

My Jesuit friends have told me that one of the oldest tricks in the book for the Roman Catholic Church is that councils and commissions will continuously quote letters and reports, even if the original document did not have any authority. Over time, if you quote such sources enough, then a document will gain authority, even authority it was never intended to have. It is sort of the case that if you say it enough times, then people will begin to believe it, no matter what. I see a little of this in the Windsor Report's use of the Virginia Report and even in its discussion of Anglican Communion canon law. So unpacking and recalling the source documents is very important. Thanks for affirming this sometimes unglamorous and time-consuming work.

PZ: So on every front, you and I are agreed here.

What do the appendices have to say about the Four Instruments, the nature of an "Anglican Covenant"?

ID: I have already spoken at length about the first two appendices, so I do not think I need to labor the point here. Suffice it to say that Appendix 1 continues the Commission's advancement of the Four Instruments of Unity as a means to keep the Anglican Communion together. I agree with you that it attempts to "tighten up" the instruments and results in giving additional power to the primates for inter-Anglican affairs. Appendix 2 is the suggested Anglican Covenant as drafted by a member or two of the Commission but not deliberated over in plenary by the whole Commission itself. The draft offers much for consideration, but we need not forget that the real import of the Commission's recommendations is that each church in the Anglican Communion adopt a brief Anglican Communion law that empowers its primate to enter into an Anglican Covenant on behalf of his (and it is "his," since all primates are currently men) church. Appendices 3 and 4 are lists of supporting documents and published works consulted by the Lambeth Commission. The real import of the appendices is thus in Appendix 1 and Appendix 2, and readers of the Windsor Report should consider with care what these two appendices are suggesting. We neglect them at our peril.

PZ: In general, the appendices tighten up the Four Instruments of Unity. Appendix Two spells out the covenant that is to be asked of each province.

In the "tightening," the ACC is regularized a bit in the area of terms of office, rolling off, coming on, and representation. The Lambeth Conference is urged to tackle more closely the meaning of episcopal authority in a corporate sense. There is also a desire to differentiate between resolutions of the Conference that have some major call on obedience and those that are more recommendations or invitations. The meeting of the primates is also now regarded as a sort of standing committee of the Lambeth Conference. This is a beefing up of things as they now stand. The Anglican Communion Office is also given the official liaison role for making the above three instruments related to the Communion as a whole. Nothing is added to the role of the Archbishop of Canterbury.

Appendix 2, giving out the covenant, is too labored and lengthy! Like ECUSA's proposed model for Delegated Episcopal Pastoral Oversight, the covenant proposed here is too detailed, too ambiguous, and too many-headed. Given the instantaneous-gratification model of contemporary life, not to mention the Americanization of the world, I cannot imagine most Provinces going through the motions to examine and affirm all the sections of this proposed covenant. It is not that the proposal offered is gobbledygook, for on its own it sounds perfectly good and proper. But it will never work. It is too subtle and too lengthy.

Here is what I think it should have said: "As a part of Christ's one, holy, catholic, and apostolic church, we promise not to do anything in the area of innovations in faith and morals without consulting with all our partners in communion." Period. That is all that is necessary, notwithstanding the theological "whereas" material backing up the first assertion of catholicity.

ID: Before leaving this part of our conversation that considers theological and ecclesiological issues in the Windsor Report, I do want to bring up one other suggestion in the report that we have not yet discussed; namely, the place and function of the Archbishop of Canterbury in Anglican Communion affairs. I am generally sympathetic to the view that the Archbishop of Canterbury, as the *primus inter pares* (first among equals), "must not be regarded as a figurehead, but as the central focus of both unity and mission within the Communion" (par. 108). For me, the history that every Anglican church shares with the See of St. Augustine (in one form or another) is an important point of common history and relationship. We are bound one to another as Anglicans through relationships, and the common relationship that we share with the Archbishop of Canterbury is central in this relational ecclesiology.

That having been said, I am a little concerned that the Windsor Report's vision of the role of the Archbishop of Canterbury favors, once again, an instrumentalist rather than a relational/missiological understanding of the office. The report suggests a new Council of Advice be created for the Archbishop of Canterbury (par. 111 and 112). The Council of Advice will "assist him (the Archbishop of Canterbury) in discerning when and how it might be appropriate for him to exercise a ministry of unity on behalf of the whole communion." The report recommends that the Council might be formed from either the Joint Standing Committees of the Anglican Consultative Council and the Primates Meeting, or even a smaller group of primates (par. 112). Regardless of who sits on the suggested Council (and it is no surprise to me that the Windsor Report suggests a significant presence of primates) the "exercise of a ministry on behalf of the whole communion" envisaged is that of adjudicating problems that arise across the Communion. Thus the new Council will not only help the Archbishop of Canterbury sit as judge, but also will, in fact, increase the expectations that Lambeth Palace can solve "problems" that arise in the Communion. I do not think that this is a good idea, and I doubt that the current incumbent of the See of Canterbury, or his staff, want to take on such new responsibilities.

PZ: There again, I like your word "relational/missional." This is a happy phrase to define our bonds of affection. Of course, under missional there is going to be some theology, and that theology I would wish to see thoroughly and even propositionally rooted in the Bible. But the theological Grace of God is surely relational. It is also certainly missional.

ID: I do believe that our only way forward in the Anglican Communion is with a relational/missional ecclesiology. And with you, this relational/missional ecclesiology needs to have an anchor in a theology grounded in the Grace of God. If the Grace of God is not relational, then I do not know what is.

PZ: Your words about the Archbishop of Canterbury are valuable, too. Like you, I wish to feel rooted in a common historical link, in an undivided "stake," as it were, in the continuity represented by Canterbury. Fortunately, we have an Archbishop in situ there who is in fact quite relational and most definitely not heavy-handed. So I have no problem with his office, and to some extent even his person, being a visible point of unity.

ID: I share your opinion about the current incumbent of the See of Canterbury. Archbishop Williams is most definitely relationally oriented and not heavy-handed. Now whether his strength of person, incredible intellect, and deep prayerfulness can withstand the forces that would like his office to exercise more central power and authority, we shall see.

Chapter 4

What Should We Do Now?

What is the report suggesting as next steps that need to be taken to "maintain communion"?

PAUL ZAHL: I would phrase this rather as "What is the report suggesting as next steps to be taken to *restore* communion"? This is because huge damage has already been done. I feel we are beyond "maintaining." Or rather, the only way now to maintain communion is to heal and restore what has been broken and been damaged. Please remember, there are scores and scores of Episcopal priests who have already left ECUSA, or been drummed out for their consorting with the Network and the AAC (i.e., American Anglican Council), as a result of 8/5/2003. Many careers have been ended, at least formally; and hundreds of thousands of people, lay and ordained, have been affected negatively by this trauma. That is no overstatement. (Just think of the airfares that have been paid out, all around the world, in direct response to the ECUSA action. Maybe it will all help US Airways to avoid bankruptcy, again!)

According to the report, the main next step to be taken is for ECUSA to express explicitly and/or liturgically its "regret that the proper constraints of the bonds of affection were breached in the events surrounding the election and consecration of a bishop for the See of New Hampshire . . . " (sec. D.134). The report also calls on those bishops who were involved with those events as protagonists to step back from further official involvement with the Communion. ECUSA, not to mention the Diocese of New Westminster, is also called upon to stop doing it. No more provocative consecrations or liturgies!

The big question is whether the carefully chosen word "regret" is strong enough. Some interpreters of the report wish to elide "regret" with the first paragraph in 134, which speaks reassuringly of "the imperatives of communion — the repentance, forgiveness and reconciliation enjoined on us by Christ." In other words, some interpreters wish to read "repent" where it says "regret." A number of "conservatives," including some members of the Commission itself, are arguing this way. I think that is wishful thinking, or something like wishful thinking. "Regret," which is used again and again in this decisive, concluding section of the Windsor Report, does not mean "repent." Moreover, even if it did mean it, the "regret" that is enjoined is only for a breaching of those famous "bonds of affection." There is no vertical dimension here — even to the effect that breaching the bonds of love is somehow a tear in our relationship to God. As ever in the report, the thing is handled horizontally, "process"-wise, rather than vertically, God's Word–and God's Grace–wise.

There is another, important part of the "next steps," too, which calls on all the bishops and archbishops from the "conservative" side who have intervened over geographical boundaries to shepherd and protect conservative congregations within ECUSA and New Westminster, to "stop what you're doing" (Beatles). These people, too, are enjoined to express their "regret" for what they have undertaken. That is problematic for "traditional" voices like my own, but more on that below.

IAN DOUGLAS: Once again, Paul, I am in agreement with you that the real question is not about how we go about "maintaining communion" but rather how do we "restore communion" across the Anglican churches worldwide, recalling though that communion maintained or restored is always a gift from God and not of our own doing.

I am also in agreement with you that repentance needs to be a key next step in the process of restoration. Repentance, however, is not a one-sided activity where only one church or a few churches are called to participate. We are all fallen individuals and communities, and each person and church in the Anglican

Communion is no different. I very much resonate with the Archbishop of Canterbury's Advent 2004 letter to the primates of the Anglican Communion, when he says: "To repent before one another is to see that we have failed in our witness as God's new community, failed to live in the full interdependence of love — and so to see that we have compromised the way in which God can make himself heard and seen among us."

Unfortunately the press has misconstrued the Archbishop's letter to say that only the Episcopal Church and the Diocese of New Westminster in Canada need to repent of our actions with respect to the full inclusion of gay men and lesbians in the life of the church. I grant you that the Episcopal Church is not always aware of and sensitive to how our decisions affect the wider world (no matter how many times sisters and brothers in Christ around the world have warned us). I'm afraid going it alone is an endemic American disease in the geopolitical realities of the world today. So I will own our culpability and agree that we as an American church need to repent of our isolation from, and lack of interdependence with, sister Anglican churches around the world. At the same time, I believe that many others in the Episcopal Church who are against the decisions of the 2003 General Convention have been able, once again because of American political, economic, and ecclesiological might, to export our issues around the world, making them the dominant church concern while millions of people suffer and die from disease, poverty, war, and interreligious conflict. So there is plenty of opportunity to repent of our American dominance and unilateralism on both sides of the homosexuality debate. And finally, the way many churches around the world have been able to play out their own power politics onto this stage of debate provides additional opportunities for repentance. Sin being what it is, none of us is free from the need of repentance.

Now before going too far into this last bit of our discussion, I want to take the opportunity to offer my own vision as to what we need to do to "maintain communion." Much of what I am going to say I published in a recent article in *The Journal of Anglican*

Studies. I want to reiterate my thoughts here, however, because I think they are germane to our discussion.

Archbishop of Canterbury Rowan Williams, speaking in a BBC interview immediately after the October 2003 extraordinary meeting of primates at Lambeth Palace, said of the current crisis in the Anglican Communion: "What complicates matters where the Anglican Church is concerned is that we're not a single monolithic body with a single decision-making authority. Our Communion depends a great deal on relationships rather than rules, and it's those relationships that are strained at the moment...." This simple yet profound statement of the Archbishop sums up many of the dynamics in current conflicts over identity and authority in the Anglican Communion. While some might advocate for a single monolithic body with a decision-making authority as a solution to our present problems (a direction I find in the Windsor Report), the real meaning of communion rests on relationships rather than rules. For communion is not so much about ecclesial structures and instruments of unity but rather about relationships, relationships across difference where commonality is found through shared service to God's mission in the world. And it is these relationships that are strained at the moment.

While recognizing that there are divisions and difficulties in Anglicanism today, the December 2003 meeting of the Inter-Anglican Standing Commission on Mission and Evangelism (IASCOME) in Jamaica (the one that I mentioned above) noted that relationships in God's mission are the basis for unity in the Body of Christ. In our Communiqué, we members of IASCOME spoke of the unity we find in mission relationships. "We were saddened that the Anglican Communion is currently living with deep tensions and disagreements over certain issues in human sexuality such that there is impaired communion between some of the churches in the Communion. Members spoke honestly about how recent actions by, and reactions to, the Episcopal Church in the United States have caused hurt, anger, and pain to many across the world and the Anglican Communion. We believe, however, that how we relate as a Communion in mission offers hope and healing to this fractured family of churches. We commit ourselves to living together in mission. We offer our stories and relationships in mission to the Anglican Communion as signs of God's transforming love." Even in the midst of pronouncements of impaired communion between some of the Anglican churches represented at IASCOME, we members of the Commission were able to bridge our differences and find common fellowship, common sharing in the Eucharistic feast, as we came together to advance the Anglican Communion's participation in and faithfulness to God's mission.

Relationships in mission, as they are described in the work of IASCOME, are predicated on the fact that Anglicans from different provinces, different cultural contexts, different social realities, can and must come together in service to God's saving action in the world. A missiological understanding of communion thus celebrates and lifts up difference as a positive expression of the wholeness of the Body of Christ. Unanimity, sameness, and homogeneity, deny the infinite possibilities that God has presented in the goodness of creation. The plurality of Anglican expressions of the gospel around the world and the differences that exist among the provinces of the Anglican Communion are a gift from God that invites us into deeper relationships with God and each other in God's mission.

Anglicanism, considered within this missiological dimension of difference, is not a monolithic globalized extension of English, or any other monocultural form of Christianity. Rather Anglicanism is the ongoing incarnational expression of the good news of Jesus Christ in an endless variety of particular cultural and social contexts that are bound together in a global family of churches through a shared history and service to God's mission. Put another way, Anglicanism is the embrace and celebration of apostolic catholicity within vernacular moments. God has embraced humanity in all of our different realities through the birth, life, death, and resurrection of Jesus Christ. Empowered by the Holy Spirit, the Body of Christ comes together to celebrate and make real the ongoing saving work of God in Christ. This embrace and celebration has continuity with the ongoing universal witness of the church throughout all time, and for Anglicans apostolicity comes through the shared story of the See of Canterbury. Yet the embrace and celebration can only be made real and experienced as the universal good news of God in Christ is translated, contextualized, in the languages, cultures, and social contexts of a variety of local realities or what I have called "vernacular moments."

Communion, in light of this rather thick theological definition of Anglicanism, is the apostolic universal sharing in the oneness of the Body of Christ across the variety of different cultural and social contexts through relationships in service to God's mission. Communion is a gift from God. It is the unity in the Body of Christ that is lived out as Anglicans, empowered by the Holy Spirit, come together across different incarnational realities to serve and advance God's mission of reconciliation and restoration. Unity in God's mission is celebrated and made real in a Eucharistic fellowship where Anglicans encounter anew God's embrace of the world through the resurrected Christ in each other around God's table. Communion is thus primarily based upon relationships of mutual responsibility and interdependence in the Body of Christ as Anglicans come together to serve God's mission in the world. Communion then is not arbitrated or advanced by structures articulating or enforcing specific legal or canonical guidelines. Rather, communion is discovered, lived into, through an infinite variety of incarnational relationships and shared experiences in service to God's mission. Missionaries serving in another province in the Anglican Communion; shared efforts and resources across Anglican churches to combat poverty, violence, HIV/AIDS and other diseases; companion diocese visits; and consultations of theologians and other groups with shared concerns are all expressions of relationships characteristic of a communion in mission.

All too often, in the rush to highlight the difficulties in the Anglican Communion today or the desire to seek resolution to such problems through structural or canonical means, the possibilities of communion in mission relationships are overlooked or neglected. Common efforts to serve God's mission of reconciliation and restoration across differences in Anglicanism offer glimpses into the possibilities for the Anglican Communion and its unity now and into the future. We need only consider the witness of Anglicans the world over in proclaiming the Good News of Christ during the Decade of Evangelism, passing significant international debt-relief legislation, or combating the scourge of HIV/AIDS to be reminded that our communion is indeed a gift from God that is made real when we serve God's mission of reconciliation and restoration in the world.

PZ: Your underlining of the fact, as I see it, that we are not seeking to "maintain" but rather to "restore" is just so exactly true. Also the fact, in true and lived experience, that "relationships" not "rules" are called for here could not be more importantly expressed.

I do want to go one further step, though, Ian, which is to say that relationships do best when they are lived out together under the common claim, upon our lives, of the Grace of God. And that comes to us powerfully — and I want to say, uniquely — from the revelation of the Bible. In other words, relationships alone are not sufficient to survive massive wounding. I noted in a recent *New York Times* (January 2, 2005) that the U.S. Army is experiencing some real success in helping stressed marriages of its soldiers who are overseas, through marriage-encounter programs rooted in the church. There has been a big upturn in military divorces as a result of the Iraq War and the prolonged separations for military families which the war has created. It was not enough to get couples just to sit down in the same room, helpful as that could be. But there had to be a "God"-dimension to the thing. And this is working, for hundreds of stressed relationships.

ID: Paul, you are, once again, absolutely correct. Relationships alone will not restore the Communion, but rather relationships that "are lived together under the common claim of the Grace of God." The goodness and love of the Grace of God in all things, in all creation, I take as the bedrock on which our lives and our faith are built — so much so that I assumed that such underlies and guides all relationships. So I have no problem at all going one step further and underscoring, or making explicit, that our relationships across difference in God's mission of reconciliation are indeed guided by, nurtured by, fostered by the Grace of God. Thanks for the reminder.

PZ: So I want to agree with you completely about the trumping of relationship over rules, absolutely. But can we not go one further step together in adding the vertical or "revealed truth" dimension to the mix, which finally binds together black and white, gay and straight, female and male, rich and poor, "master and servant" (Depeche Mode), and all the other dividednesses of the human condition? That is all I would add to what you have richly written.

ID: Now as to the "revealed truth dimension to the mix," you and I have already been down this path in our conversation. Yes, I believe that the word of God in the New and the Old Testament contains all things necessary for salvation. And I do believe that the Holy Scriptures are the true and authoritative guide for a life of faith. I think you and I agree that we are on solid and common ground here. What I think you and I agree to disagree on, however, is whether the Bible has spoken once and for all on matters related to homosexuality, as we know such in our current contemporary context. While we might disagree about this, I trust that the Grace of God which is at the heart of our relationship in Christ will continue to bind you and me together as we continue to seek our way forward in these difficult and confusing times. Thanks be to God.

What is it saying about elections to the episcopate, generally across the Communion and in the Episcopal Church?

PZ: Clearly the report is saying, Cease and Desist! ECUSA is being called on to honor a complete moratorium on the election and consecration of actively gay homosexuals to the episcopate. Troubling to me is the added phrase "until some new consensus in the Anglican Communion emerges" (sec. D.134). That leaves the door open to a "change of heart" on the part of the whole Communion, possibly at the Lambeth Conference being planned for 2008. On this question, "traditionalists" would be much happier with the door closed on such a possibility, definitely and cleanly. It is a subject on which Bible-Christians are not able to change their minds. Not because we are dinosaurs — but because we believe God has already spoken. We will be regarded as troglodytes for saying this — after all, is the face behind the Wizard of Oz simply our *own* human face and not the true face of Revelation? Well, that is the standard charge. But it is a secular and humanistic charge. Neither the Roman Catholics nor the evangelical/ Pentecostal Protestants will ever change their minds on this particular point. Remember, I wish it were not so. "Say it isn't so" (Hall and Oates).

ID: Yes, there is no way around it. The Windsor Report does take the position of, in your words, "Cease and Desist." The Lambeth Commission, particularly in the way that the report singles out the Bishop of New Hampshire, says that no church in the Anglican Communion should elect, appoint, ordain, or consecrate to the episcopate "a person in an openly acknowledged same gender union" (par. 129). Note, however, that the commission did not say that a homosexual person who is living a celibate life is fundamentally ruled out from being a bishop in the church, but rather only those living "in an openly acknowledged same gender union." If the Commission were to take a position on celibate homosexual people in the episcopate, then it would have to consider other churches in the Anglican Communion beyond the Episcopal Church. Instead the Lambeth Commission concentrated only on the case of New Hampshire and the Episcopal Church USA.

I am in agreement with you that the Windsor Report does leave open the door that, perhaps some time in the future, a person living in an openly acknowledged same-gender union might be an acceptable candidate for the episcopate. The phrase "until some new consensus in the Anglican Communion emerges" does not at all bother me as it does you (par. 134). Then again, I am not in the same place as you on the finality of biblical pronouncements related to questions of human sexuality, and homosexuality in particular. I do want to acknowledge, however, that the "until" is troublesome for you. Still, given the work of the Holy Spirit, I believe that all things are possible, and I would want to sit more provisionally with what the future might or might not hold for the church. You are correct, perhaps our next conversation should be about the Holy Spirit?

Much is being made of paragraph 134 and the specific recommendations to the Episcopal Church in light of the election, consent, and consecration of the Bishop of New Hampshire. As you can imagine this is the paragraph that most people in the Episcopal Church will focus on without necessarily reading the whole report. I think this is a mistake, as there are many other substantive issues afoot in the report, as we have noted in our conversation so far. That having been said, I do want to make a few points of clarification about paragraph 134. We have already discussed the need for repentance that goes beyond regret in the face of the "breaching of the constraints of the bonds of affection." I think the larger focus on repentance is the right note to strike. But as I have already noted, there is much room for repentance on all sides. Second, there seems to be a lot of conversation in the Episcopal Church about how bishops who participated in the consecration of Bishop Robinson should immediately "withdraw themselves from representative functions in the Anglican Communion." This overlooks the provisional statement: "pending such expression of regret." I would also like more specifics as to which representative functions are in the minds of the Commissioners. I'm afraid that many interpreters of this point in paragraph #134 are all too quick to point fingers and exclude without serious consideration as to who and what is implied.

Finally, I think the Lambeth Commission in paragraph 134 showed that they really do not understand the democratic representative polity of the Episcopal Church. How exactly is the Episcopal Church to "effect a moratorium on the election and consent to the consecration of any candidate to the episcopate who is living in a same gender union"? I guess each diocesan nomination process for an episcopal election could respect this admonition and decide among themselves to not put forward such a candidate. Or individuals who are voting in a diocesan election could take these words to heart as they discern how to cast their vote if, in fact, there was a candidate living in a same-gender union. Or I guess the House of Bishops could pass a "mind-of-the-house resolution" saying that diocesan bishops agree not to give their consent to a person living in a same-gender union, if and when such a person was elected. There is even some talk of bishops agreeing among themselves not to give consent to any Episcopal elections, be they of heterosexual or homosexual persons! Mind-of-the-house resolutions, however, pertain only to the bishops and are not canonically binding. In my view of the polity of the Episcopal Church, the only way that such a moratorium could be effected is if both the House of Deputies and the House of Bishops passed a canon at a General Convention specifically saying that a person living in a same-gender union is not eligible to be a candidate for the episcopate. So as much as I understand the sentiment behind paragraph 134, I think the polity implications are much more complicated.

PZ: As my friend the Lutheran theologian Rod Rosenbladt observes, how odd and seemingly almost eccentric that St. Paul should have focused on this sin during the opening of his theological argument in Romans. Why not take any number of other sins? Why major on this particular phenomenon? Why this particular color in the mosaic of human forlornness and lovelessness and compensatory use? Why, I ask? We have not been given to know. So I rest in its profundity, and also its mystery. Bible-people, to use John Stott's phrase, can honestly, and vulnerably, do no other.

In any event, the report is a definite no to further elections and consecrations along this line. I think this is good. Most of us on the "traditional" side think this is good. We are only troubled by that added "until."

What is it saying about Rites of Blessing of same-sex unions generally across the Communion and in the Episcopal Church?

PZ: "Second verse, same as the first" ("Henry the Eighth" — Herman's Hermits). In other words, the same message is given concerning these rites as is given concerning actively gay bishops: Cease and Desist!

ID: Yes, the Windsor Report takes the same position "on Public Rites of Blessing of same sex unions" that it does on the election of and consecration to the episcopate of individuals living in openly acknowledged same-gender unions. The position, as you have said, Paul, is "Cease and Desist." While there was the "until some new consensus in the Anglican Communion emerges" clause in the episcopate question (par. 134), this section on Public Rites of Blessing of same-sex unions calls on the supporters of blessings of same-sex unions actively to make a theological case for such. The report says: "the churches proposing to take action must be able, as a beginning, to demonstrate to the rest of the Communion why their proposal meets the criteria of scripture, tradition, and reason. In order to be received as a legitimate development of the tradition, it must be possible to demonstrate how public Rites of Blessing for same sex unions would constitute growth in harmony with the apostolic tradition as it has been received" (par. 141). It seems as if the Commission is asking for more theological justification as to why the church should head in this direction. The proponents for the Rites of Blessing for same-sex unions thus have their work cut out for them.

More striking for me, however, is the fact that the Windsor Report has completely misinterpreted the actions of the 2003 General Convention with respect to Rites of Blessing for same-sex unions. The report says that the Convention "decided to allow experimentation with public Rites of Blessing of same sex unions" (par. 27), "commended the development of public Rites of Blessing for same sex unions" (par. 140), took actions that "move towards the authorization of such rites" (par. 141), and "made provision for the development of public Rites of Blessing of same sex unions" (par. 144). As much as those in favor of, and also against, the blessings of same-sex unions might hope that the 2003 General Convention took such actions as those described in the Windsor Report, the fact is the Convention did not allow experimentation with, commend the development of, move towards the authorization of, or make provision for "public Rites of Blessing of same sex unions."

Reviewing the legislative record of the 2003 General Convention, one finds that the original text of resolution C051 on "Committed Same-Gender Relationships" sought to "approve the liturgical blessing of the committed relationship of two adults of the same gender and authorize the inclusion of such blessing in the 'Book of Occasional Services.'" The House of Bishops, however, did not advance this resolution. Rather a substitute resolution was passed by both the House of Bishops and the House of Deputies that included eight descriptive pastoral points, including: "That in keeping with the Pastoral Letter from the Primates of the Anglican Communion (5/27/03) 'acknowledging the responsibility of Christian leaders to attend to the pastoral needs of minorities in their care'; we recognize that local faith communities are operating within the bounds of our common life as they explore and experience liturgies celebrating and blessing same-sex union."

I believe that the substitute C051 resolution was more descriptive as compared to the more proscriptive original C051 resolution. In my opinion, the Lambeth Commission has completely misunderstood the intent of General Convention 2003. The Rt. Rev. Paul V. Marshall, Bishop of the Diocese of Bethlehem, Pennsylvania, who was closely connected with the C051 legislation, confirms my view. He has written: "The (Lambeth) commission's characterization of the 2003 General Convention as authorizing the creation of same-sex rites seems, unavoidably, to be a willful misrepresentation. As the sole author of General Convention's offending paragraph, which was discussed in public committee meeting before coming publicly to the floor, I know that the text was designed to say that while the church *cannot* now authorize such rites, it can tolerate their existence, giving the Spirit room to work and teach us one way or the other. To tolerate is different than to authorize; a document (the Windsor Report) generally careful about definitions disappoints by nodding here." I think giving the Holy Spirit room to work and teach us one way or the other is not a bad direction to take.

PZ: In some ways, the section on same-sex unions reads a little stronger than the section which precedes it. I like this part especially: " . . . it would be true to say that very many people within the Communion fail to see how the authorisation of such a rite is compatible with the teaching of scripture, tradition and reason. In such circumstances, it should not be surprising that such developments are seen by some as surrendering to the spirit of the age rather than an authentic development of the gospel." Way to go! Most of us, probably all of us, on the "traditional" side have believed all along that ECUSA is conceding way too much to the Zeitgeist in its new affirmed sexual ethic. We have felt we have watched as the denomination has proven to be vulnerable to what the megaphones in the world are insisting on. We have wanted the church to be true to its authentically counterintuitive and deconstructing legacy: the gospel message of repentance, grace, and faith. When ECUSA tumbled over the edge, on 8/5/2003, we believed to our toes that ECUSA had become *the* conformist church of the time. I remembered that Bertolucci film *The Conformist,* in which a man morphs in and out of fascism, communism, and even Judaism for a flash, and the center to the character is so painfully hollow. This is how we see our church today.

So we like that paragraph concerning "the spirit of the age." I only wish that it had been phrased a little more activistically and less as if the "very many people within the Communion" were sort of a Margaret Mead experiment in anthropology. "Conservatives" often feel that we are regarded as a "phenomenon" to be studied (and condescended to), rather than real people. This, one could argue, is why the recent U.S. presidential election turned out the way it did.

What is it saying about the "care of dissenting groups" of same-sex unions generally across the Communion and in the Episcopal Church?

ID: I am not at all surprised by the Windsor Report's endorsement of traditional understandings of geographic jurisdictional authority of bishops (par. 148 and 154). This is in keeping with the generally "conserving of tradition" ethic of the report. When all is said and done, I think that the majority of those in power (and I mean bishops here) will want to protect the diocesan power that they have, no matter what side they might be on the hot-button issues related to human sexuality. Interestingly enough, the only folk that I see in the Anglican Communion who are looking at other organizational models for the diocese beyond that of geographic jurisdictions are a few "postmodern" thinkers (many of whom are "conservative" on the sexuality issues) and certain cultural/ethnic groups for whom the geographic jurisdictional model never really fit in the first place.

PZ: Here the Windsor Report loses the plot entirely. Here, in the to-us-traditionalists-extremely-important section concerning the care of dissenting groups, the report breaks down in all plausibility and helpfulness. Interestingly, this is the first section to which almost all North American traditionalists turned when the report was published on the eighteenth of October. And here we felt let down.

What the Commission does is to affirm in toto the proposal for DEPO (i.e., Delegated Episcopal Pastoral Oversight) that was conceived by the ECUSA House of Bishops at a meeting in Texas during March of last year. We rejected it then as we reject it now. Why? Because the people most directly affected, the dissenting minorities in mainstream ECUSA dioceses, were not directly consulted. This is not to avoid the criticism, which traditionalist bishops received then, that by many of them boycotting the meeting they lost their right both to make an impact and to complain later. But their boycotting was justifiable in many ways. Those meetings of the ECUSA House of Bishops had become festivals in the triumph of "process" over substance, and the "design" of the meetings, to quote a favorite word, had been so to break up any serious resistance to the tide as it was going, that "traditional" bishops simply lost heart. It was never actually possible, from all direct reports from "conservatives," to actually discuss anything in real terms. Everything was "conversation," "break out" groups, intermingling of every viewpoint so that no single viewpoint could be actively registered. The result was always this: dissenters felt silenced. No wonder many of our traditional bishops felt alienated and disheartened. Utterly.

ID: In addition, I am not surprised by, and actually I am very sympathetic to, the call to recognize and care for "dissenting groups" who are seeking to be faithful members of the Anglican family (par. 150). This, I think, shows some genuine pastoral concern for those who feel as if they are becoming strangers in their own church. I do hear the pain in your words, and they reflect just how hurt "dissenting groups" can feel in the midst of all of this ecclesial turmoil.

I must say, however, that I am surprised that the report unreservedly commends the Delegated Episcopal Pastoral Oversight plan (DEPO) as developed by the House of Bishops of the Episcopal Church in March 2004. The fact that the Lambeth Commission would move the language from "alternative Episcopal oversight," as issued in the communiqué from the 2003 October meeting of the primates at Lambeth Palace, to "delegated pastoral oversight" signals that the Commission believes that the leadership of the Episcopal Church has responded appropriately to the care of dissenting groups (par. 151 and 152).

I do not share your opinion that "dissenting minorities in mainstream ECUSA dioceses were not directly consulted" about Delegated Pastoral Episcopal Oversight. Such bishops might have voluntarily absented themselves from meetings of the House of Bishops where DEPO was discussed, but a choice not to participate does not qualify as being excluded from the conversation. In my mind, you have to be there if you want to participate. Neither do I agree with your estimation that the meetings of the House of Bishops of the Episcopal Church have "become festivals in the triumph of 'process' over substance, and the 'design' of the meetings had been so to break up any serious resistance to the tide." I think you know that since mid-2001 I have been working as a consultant to the Presiding Bishop and House of Bishops in their mission education and global reconciliation efforts. As a consultant, I have attended every meeting of the House of Bishops in toto or in part since September 2001 and have also participated in many of the planning sessions for the meetings. I can say that in all of my work with the bishops over the last four years, I have never seen anyone try to manipulate the design of the meetings "to break up any serious resistance to the tide," as you say. You seem to be advancing a conspiracy theory here, where I, frankly, refuse to see one. In my experience with the House of Bishops, I have found that every bishop and staff person associated with the design, planning, and implementation of the meetings has done their utmost to make sure that all sides on any one question are well aired in an open and transparent manner. (And I might add here that there are bishops involved in the planning and direction for the House of Bishops who are on opposite sides of the homosexuality question and who voted for and voted against the consent for the Bishop of New Hampshire.) What I do not find in those involved with the planning and direction of the House of Bishops are strident bishops who represent ends of the spectrum in any contentious question or on the hot-button issue. I can say that I have been incredibly blessed by my work with the bishops since 2001, and I have found, by and large, that the vast majority of bishops in the House are people of deep faith who love Jesus and genuinely care for the whole church. I am genuinely impressed by the work the bishops have done together over the last four years, particularly in their understanding of and commitment to God's mission.

PZ: What the ECUSA bishops should have done is appointed a group of "traditionalists" to make a united statement of what we need. Not what "they" want us to need, or think we should need in order not to be "congregationalists" (the one unforgivable sin in the American setting), but what we need. What we need in order to feel safe. Several of us had approached the Presiding Bishop with a proposal that he deputize a conservative bishop friendly to the aggrieved minority — "our" appointment, you might say, not his idea of who our appointment should be, but "our appointment" — and delegate to that bishop the pastoral oversight of all the Network and other clergy and parishes, on terms to which they could agree, for two years, say. And let that be an attempted renewal of trust and trust-level. Give it a sort of "concession to the 'losers' " status, for a definite period, in hopes that feelings would subside and honor be shown to "the weaker brethren." But no. This was not granted. Rather, the regnant side told the disheartened side what it would give and not give. Plus, they presented us with a process that only a lawyer in Bleak House would have the patience, let alone the mastery of small print, to prosecute. The whole thing is and was hopelessly unworkable, certainly in the American context, where waiting is just about impossible to conceive and results are flashed with the click of a keyboard. So the "Camp Allen" plan, which the Windsor Report now endorses, was a nonstarter from the absolute beginning.

ID: Returning to the specifics of the Windsor Report, there seems to be a kind of parallel drawn, with respect to the actions now required of the "perpetrators," between those who supported the election and consecration of a bishop living in a same-sex relationship and that of episcopal diocesan boundary crossing. Expression of regret, affirmation of desire to remain in communion, and effecting of a moratorium are presented as necessary next steps (par. 155). I know that those who have advocated and participated in boundary crossing argue that making their actions on par with the election and consecration of the Bishop of New Hampshire is a gross overrepresentation of their actions. They thus take offense at the implied moral equivalency of the acts. I find it interesting, however, that those who are called to a moratorium on the election and consent to the consecration of any candidate to the episcopate of any person living in a same-gender relationship and a moratorium on the public Rite of Blessing for same-sex unions, and those who are being asked for a moratorium on the crossing of diocesan boundaries, all believe that they are morally correct in their actions and take offense at what the Windsor Report is asking. To my ears both sides sound strikingly similar in their responses to the recommendations of the Windsor Report.

PZ: To add vinegar to the wound, the Eames Commission now calls upon "those diocesan bishops of the Episcopal Church (USA) who have refused to countenance the proposals set out by their House of Bishops to reconsider their own stance on this matter. If they refuse to do so, in our view, they will be making a profoundly dismissive statement about their adherence to the polity of their own church" (sec. D.155).

Now that is simply too bad a reversal of the power dynamic at work here. Having taken away what little sense of autonomy the "losers" (in ECUSA terms) have, those exact losers are to apologize for responding with the only means at their disposal to respond. Take away the rights we have, then tell us not to respond from the heart! And set the crossing of geographical boundaries on a par of equivalence with an innovation in faith and morals that is infinitely more corrosive and depleting.

The last paragraph — it is section D.155 — in the Windsor Report is the low point. I felt that my old and true friends, the bishops whom almost all in the "dissenting minorities" regard as the demeaned upholders of the catholic faith of God's Grace within ECUSA, are now lectured in some kind of attempt to sound even-handed yet within a church context that is going entirely one way: the other way.

ID: Finally, I am very surprised that you and I read the Commission's call upon "diocesan bishops of the Episcopal Church who have refused to countenance the proposals set out by their House of Bishops to reconsider their stance on the matter" as speaking to two different constituencies (par. 155). You think that this paragraph is speaking to the "boundary crossers" with whom you are sympathetic and thus experience this as "adding vinegar to the wound." I argue that this injunction is aimed at those diocesan bishops who are refusing to implement Delegated Episcopal Pastoral Oversight for "conservative" parishes in their dioceses. (And these are indeed very few in number.) My textual clue for this position is that the Commission specifically identifies Episcopal Church *diocesan* bishops, and the only bishops that I know of who have crossed boundaries are either retired bishops or bishops from other churches in the Anglican Communion. So the injunction to "diocesan bishops of the Episcopal Church who have refused to countenance the proposals set out by their House of Bishops" clearly means those who are refusing to implement DEPO. I'm afraid that the hurt you feel has somewhat blinded you from the sometimes subtle words of the report. I hope my clarification here helps to wash away some of the vinegar in your wounds.

Are these recommendations enough, too little, too harsh, and why?

PZ: My answer to the last question is probably predictable, Ian. The recommendations are too little. Enjoining a moratorium on homosexual bishops is good, at least from where I am coming from. Ditto the moratorium on same-sex unions. The care for dissenting minorities, however, is completely co-opted against the people it claims to want to help. In my view, the heroes are the CAPA bishops in Africa, who have affirmed the Network and supported the troubled consciences of the "traditionalists." And there are many other such bishops, throughout worldwide Anglicanism, who are with those.

   The Windsor Report could have gone just 20 percent further in order to make a lasting, healing difference — had they thrown in their lot and heartfelt sympathy with the complainants, both in the Two-Thirds World and in North America, and simply enjoined ECUSA to respond concessively to the losers. The word here is "concession." The Commission should have enjoined ECUSA to make dramatic concessions to those who are so disheartened and discouraged by the 8/5/2003 move that they can scarcely look up. In Philippians 2 terms, the power people in ECUSA need to stoop, and give it all up, to the losers, so the losers, the "weaker brethren" in their view but now the truly weakened brethren, can look back up, upon the face of Grace. The power people need do this, and they could do this, because we all believe in God. We believe that in giving, we always, by the power of the Holy Spirit, receive.

ID: You are correct here, Paul; I could have predicted that you would support the moratorium on the election and consecration of bishops living in same-sex relationships and the moratorium on the public Rites of Blessing for same-sex unions while dissenting from the moratorium on diocesan boundary crossing for the care of dissenting minorities. I do understand how you wish that the Commission would have gone 20 percent further by affirming those who have "supported the troubled consciences of the 'traditionalists.'" This implies that you have got 80 percent of what you wanted.

You and I both know that the Commission, especially given the makeup of the group, had widely held divergent positions on many of the topics we have been discussing. We also know that if any one side had been able to get 100 percent of what they wanted, then the Windsor Report would not have been offered unanimously. In such a circumstance, I assume that a "minority report" would have been offered from the "losing side." This would have been, in my estimation, quite sad, for a nonunanimous report would allow many across the Anglican Communion to discount the findings of the Lambeth Commission as being too one-sided. So I am not at all surprised by and am quite sympathetic to the attempt by the Lambeth Commission to deal evenhandedly with all sides. By and large I think they have succeeded in this, even if it means that no one will be ultimately pleased with, or get everything they wanted in, the report.

PZ: Right now, unfortunately, the Episcopal Church is like Reconstruction in the American South after 1865. The losers, to whom

President Lincoln intended to be so kind and gracious and genuinely concessive, were ground to powder by a far less forgiving
administration than Lincoln's would have been. And people who
are ground down become suppressed and sublimated in their nor-
mal (and I concede, unsanctified) feelings of hurt and anger. Grace
can go so far! What is missing in the Windsor Report is an injunction to the victors in North America to "try a little tenderness"
(Otis Redding). Do you remember listening to that *great* R & B
standby? Has its truly soulful plea ever been bettered? I mean,
tell me: Has it? Try a little tenderness. This is the concluding note
that I miss in the Eames Report. If it were there, it would make
all the difference. Since it is not, we are dealing with a text that
is a day late and a dollar short.

   Oh, but maybe the primates will still right the thing.

ID: I am taken aback by your closing hope that the primates may
     "still right the thing." I know that you think that the Anglican
     Communion is teetering on the brink of oblivion and that some-
     thing needs to be done to address the crisis. But after all that
     we have talked about with respect to our shared concerns over
     the centralization of authority in the Anglican Communion, your
     final petition to the primates leads me to wonder if you really are
     as worried about the centralization of authority in the Anglican
     Communion as I am. I know I am flogging what is coming to be
     a very old horse here, but, like you, the Windsor Report wants
     to give the very last word to the primates. The report's conclud-
     ing paragraphs are words of caution, with almost a veiled threat
     that "should the call to halt and find ways of continuing in our
     present communion not be heeded, then we shall have to begin
     to walk apart" (par. 157). Rather than giving the final word to
     Scripture, as in the quote from Ephesians 4:3 in the penultimate
     sentence, the Lambeth Commission instead gives the final say to
     the primates when they wrote in 2000 "to turn from one another
     would be to turn away from the Cross." This, I think, is sym-
     bolic of how the Windsor Report wants to give preeminence to
     the Primates Meeting, along with the other Instruments of Unity,
     in this "exercise in containment."

I hear your invitation to "try a little tenderness," and I very much support the sentiment. I think there is a great opportunity across this wonderful and wide family of churches with which you and I are privileged to be a part for an exercise of tenderness on many, many sides. There is so much hurt in our churches, and in our world for that matter, that a little tenderness will go a long way. In addition to sentiments of tenderness, I think all of us in the Anglican Communion need to look beyond ourselves, our hurts, our divisions to what it is that binds us together. For we are called "to serve and signify God's mission to the world, that mission whereby God brings to men and women, to human societies and to the whole world, real signs and foretastes of that healing love which one day will put all things to rights" (par. 3). To me this conversation has indeed been a real sign and foretaste of that love grounded in the *missio Dei* by which all things are put right. I thank you and I thank God for this gift of communion and the bonds of affection we share. Amen.

Chapter 5

LAST THOUGHTS

PAUL ZAHL: I am so heartfeltedly pleased that we have been able to come together on many fronts during the course of our conversation about the Windsor Report. We have differed on the relative weights we attach to the subject of homosexuality as it affects the life of the church and also, to a somewhat lesser extent, on the interpretation of the Bible. We have agreed on a relational model of church unity rather than a hierarchical model — this is for sure! — and we have also been united on the priority of mission and the underwriting of mission by the Holy Spirit. I myself would go a step further than the relational model, which is to say that for me the place of Scripture, or revealed authority through the Word, even trumps relationship, or rather enables relationship in the profoundest way. I am not sure you would disagree with me in this.

We have both expressed caution about the Windsor Report in its emphasis on external and/or primatial and centralized authority in the Anglican Communion. We are both also suspect of the Commission's recourse to "canon law" and any sort of legal structures to implement discipline. We find this to be an innovation in Anglicanism worldwide. Here, too, our shared Americanness makes us distrustful, extremely distrustful, of prelacy and anything that sounds like prelacy.

The main learning for me has been the very large swaths of agreement that we have discovered in our back-and-forth. The agreement has increased between us rather than decreased. This amazes me, and delights me.

So over and out — in the confidence that we could move forward together, and that what the world now calls "conversation" can happen when it is not just a notion but actually a real and experienced fact.

This encounter has given me some very serious and deep hope.

Yet let me add one further note concerning our hope of common ground and reconciling fellowship. I have had to think quite purposefully in recent months about the angularity of the so-called orthodox or conservatives in the church. Why are they — why are we! — so touchy? Why do we come across as aggressive and angry in our position-taking since and even before the vote on Gene Robinson? Well, the fact is, we are pretty aggressive and angry. And it is not picturesque.

But the cause of this unpretty picture lies in the fact that orthodox voices in the Episcopal Church have felt and have actually been marginalized for a pretty long time. I remember thirty years ago being struck with the fact that Evangelicals in the Church of England seemed to be much better assimilated in England than Evangelicals, and charismatics, were in ECUSA back in my own country. My personal experience reflected this. Sharply. To be Bible-quoting in the Episcopal Church was to be regarded as "Baptist," full stop. Episcopalians were so busy not being "evangelical" in any way, shape, or form that "born again" types coming through the church were considered to be utterly alien. This is the way it truly was. It is the way it has been. And it is the way it threatens to stay.

This is not at all good. When people are regarded as thoroughly outré, they become thoroughly outré. When they are accepted, to use the (true) cliché, they become acceptable. This is a truth of psychology. It is also a truth of faith.

I am absolutely convinced that on the day when "orthodox" voices are not written off and squeezed out of preferment and seminary training and candidacy for holy orders — which they have been in the majority of Episcopal settings, and we are paying this price now — on that day the orthodox will be able to become team players again.

This word comes from my heart. I am the dean and president of an extremely controversial entity, Trinity Episcopal School for

Ministry. Over decades I have heard bishops and diocesan ordination officers say time and time again, We will send students to Trinity — over my dead body! No kidding. Now that kind of thinking and acting creates terrible reaction. It creates the fleshly work of bitterness. It creates unabreacted rage. And then such rage gets acted out.

For myself, I would wish to help draw Trinity School back towards the mainstream of Anglican life. But I am not sure this is possible in the Episcopal Church in which I have grown up and served. Could we say this: ECUSA needs to repent, not of something — say, Gene Robinson's consecration — which has been recently done; but rather, of a mind-set that has been undeviatingly dismissive of "simple" heartfelt faith in the Old, Old Story and in its Book? I think our church *does* need to repent of this. The church has failed, pure and simple, to decide to accept as its own, doctrinaire Anglo-Catholics and charismatic Evangelicals, and John-Stott-style Evangelicals. The church has essentially said to us, de facto, Depart from me, I never knew ye.

Now *that* attitude is worth repenting of. And that spirit of meekness, before a long-term past hurt and wound, could open things up in a most important way.

Ian Douglas, I thank you for such a spirit of meekness. For it, for you, I am most thoroughly grateful.

IAN DOUGLAS: Paul, once again we find ourselves in the deepest of agreement, both on your synopsis of our conversation, and interestingly on the way that the "margins" are treated in the Episcopal Church.

Let me take the latter first. I appreciate and have even witnessed how "orthodox" or "conservatives" have been treated as "outré" in the Episcopal Church of late. I am so sorry that this has occurred, and if I have been party to or culpable in the marginalization of you or your colleagues, I want to say I repent of such and want to amend my ways. Please do hold me accountable for such amendment of life.

Interestingly though, what you say about how the Episcopal Church has regarded Trinity Episcopal School for Ministry. I have also experienced the exact same behavior with regard to the Episcopal Divinity School. Yes, I have heard bishops and Commissions on Ministry say to me, "We will send students to EDS—over my dead body." And I agree with you that such exclusivity and narrow-mindedness creates hurt, bitterness, and even, as you say, "rage." The lumps we have taken at EDS as we have tried to be faithful to God's mission of justice, compassion, and reconciliation are indeed palpable.

I have always said that Episcopal Divinity School and Trinity Episcopal School for Ministry have more in common than meets the eye. Sure, we have distinctly different theological perspectives and traditions, and I frankly celebrate theses differences and believe that both are well represented in the history and tradition of Anglicanism. While acknowledging these important differences, I find that we are very similar in that both of our schools believe that God has a vision, a mission, for the world and our passion to that vision (clearly articulated differently in Cambridge and Ambridge) drives our respective seminary curricula, worshiping life, and community cultures. Because we are mission driven and not so much ecclesially driven, our student bodies tend to be much more representative of the whole people of God and not made up primarily of those preparing for ordination in the Episcopal Church. EDS and TESM are also similar in that it "costs" our students to come to our seminaries. Our graduates cannot assume that they will be welcome in all corners of the Episcopal Church, and some parts of the church will in fact be overtly hostile to what we represent. Also, EDS and TESM have a decidedly global perspective in what we do. Both of our seminaries appreciate that the mission of God that we are dedicated to has worldwide ramifications, and thus we are profoundly committed to supporting and engaging the Anglican Communion in our educational endeavors.

So the 'bridges (Cambridge and Ambridge) are more alike than they are different, and I can empathize deeply with your description of how the orthodox/conservatives treat each other and are treated by the church. We in the progressive end of the church are not immune from the same behavior. Perhaps that is why you and I seem to get along so well together.

As to the Windsor Report, what more can I say? You have so wonderfully and succinctly noted some of our points of deep agreement, namely: the embrace of the relational model of church unity rather than the hierarchical model, the priority of the *missio Dei* and the underwriting of mission by the Holy Spirit as basic to Communion, concern over the slide to the centralization of authority in the primates or any other form of prelacy, our suspicion about the recourse to canon law and any sort of structures to implement discipline, and the affirmation that in conversation we have the confidence that we (and the whole Anglican Communion) can and must move forward together in God's mission. These and many other points of commonality have weaved themselves throughout this conversation.

Thus, there is nothing more to say than: Thank you. Thank you, Paul, for being willing to risk yourself in this venture. Thank you, Paul, for your honest and heartfelt responses to my offerings and ideas. I have felt buoyed up and supported throughout this discourse. I am eternally grateful to you and God for the possibility to share at such a deep level. I hope and pray that our conversation across the divide represents for the Episcopal Church and the broader Anglican Communion one example of how we can be bound together in mutual affection. I thank God for the bonds of affection that exist between us and offer them in service to God's mission of reconciliation for the Episcopal Church, the Anglican Communion, and the wider world. *Deo Gratias.*

A SUMMARY OF THE REPORT AND ITS CONTEXT

Jan Nunley

INTRODUCTION

The worldwide family of churches known as the Anglican Communion, tracing their origins to the Church of England and their spirituality to its Book of Common Prayer and the English Bible, holds itself together with "bonds of affection" rather than a common confession of faith or central curia. Its ability to do so is a source of some pride for a group that sees itself as a "middle way" between Christianity's extremes, and generally values theological comprehensiveness over doctrinal uniformity.

Occasionally, though, conflicts between Anglicans emerge into public view. Over the last forty years, issues such as the ordination of women as priests and bishops, changes in Prayer Book language, and the role of sexual minorities in the churches of the Communion have disturbed its peace. But these are not at the core of the ongoing dispute. Its ultimate source is a deep-seated battle over authority — who has it, how it is exercised, and in what circumstances it should be invoked.

The latest chapter in the ongoing disagreement over Anglican authority began with two events: the authorization by a diocese in Canada of a public Rite of Blessing for Same Sex Unions, and the decision by a majority of bishops with jurisdiction in the Episcopal Church to join its House of Deputies in consenting to the election of the Rev. Canon V. Gene Robinson — a noncelibate priest in a committed relationship with another man — as bishop coadjutor of New Hampshire.

Within moments of that vote, on August 5, 2003, in Minneapolis, Minnesota, conservatives in both houses opposed to the action were holding news conferences and calling on the primates — the chief archbishops or bishops — of the other thirty-seven provinces of the Anglican Communion to "intervene in the pastoral emergency that has overtaken us."[1]

Episcopal Church Presiding Bishop Frank Griswold told news reporters following the vote that he would be in contact with his fellow primates, and assured them that Archbishop of Canterbury Rowan Williams was "profoundly aware" of differing contexts within the various provinces and sensitive to the strains within the Anglican Communion over sexuality.[2]

The next day, August 6, Williams's office released a statement saying that the American decision would "inevitably have a significant impact on the Anglican Communion throughout the world," but that he hoped the churches of the Communion would reflect more deeply "before significant and irrevocable decisions are made in response."[3]

By the end of the week Williams had called an "extraordinary meeting" of the primates in London for October 15–16, 2003.

"I am clear that the anxieties caused by recent developments have reached the point where we will need to sit down and discuss their consequences," Williams said. "I hope that in our deliberations we will find that there are ways forward in this situation which can preserve our respect for one another and for the bonds that unite us."[4]

But even before the meeting convened, Robin Eames — Archbishop of Armagh, the senior primate of the Anglican Communion and a veteran of turf wars in conflict-ridden Ireland — raised questions in a September 2003 editorial in the *Church of Ireland Gazette* that framed the debate for the Primates. The confirmation of Robinson's election "has provoked a crisis for the Anglican Communion," Eames said — but not on the issue of homosexuality. Instead, the crisis regarded "the nature of unity and relationships of the diverse Provinces which make up the Communion" — the same questions which a commission headed by Eames had addressed on the issue of women's ordination in 1988.

My experience then and since has convinced me that the fundamental issue for our Communion is: How do we live together with differing opinions, differing cultures but maintain some semblance of active communion? I believe Anglicanism will survive this current controversy. The question is: in what form? ... To put it plainly — if no constitutional or legal rules exist for what constitutes membership of the Anglican Communion there are no rules for expulsion of a member Church.

...Laws apart, opinions apart and sensitivities apart diversity of culture, practice and life-styles have been and will most likely continue to be the experience of a world family such as the Anglican Communion. Perhaps the main question arising for us at this time is simply: How do we live with and how do we understand difference?[5]

The Primates Meeting, established in 1978, was originally designed by then-Archbishop Donald Coggan as a gathering for "leisurely thought, prayer and deep consultation." But "leisurely thought" has not been part of their agenda for several years. The group officially holds only an advisory status in the Anglican Communion, though several successive Lambeth Conferences — the once-a-decade gathering of Anglican bishops — have called for "enhanced responsibility" for the meeting.[6]

In a statement issued at the end of their October meeting, the primates expressed a commitment to cooperation in spite of disagreements on homosexuality. But they also reaffirmed as "the traditional teaching of the Communion" Resolution 1.10 of the 1998 Lambeth Conference, which had rejected homosexual practice as "incompatible with Scripture" and stated that the bishops could not "advise the legitimising or blessing of same sex unions nor ordaining those involved in same gender unions."[7]

"This reaffirmation means that the wider Communion cannot support the recent developments for the blessings of same sex unions or the election of Canon Gene Robinson as Bishop of New Hampshire. Indeed, the ministry of Gene Robinson as a bishop will not be recognised or received in the vast majority of the Anglican world," said an explanatory news release from the Rev. Gregory K. Cameron, director of ecumenical affairs and studies (and later deputy secretary general) for the Anglican Communion Office.[8]

As a result, Cameron said, "a state of impaired or broken Communion is beginning to exist between many parts of the Anglican world" and the Diocese of New Westminster in Canada and the Diocese of New Hampshire — and "possibly with the whole of the Episcopal Church (USA)." (The term "impaired" was in fact used in a 1988 Lambeth resolution establishing the Eames Commission on the ordination of women.[9])

The "nature, extent and duration of this impaired or broken communion" were unclear to the primates, especially given the somewhat fuzzy definition of membership in the Anglican Communion itself. "Will a breach in Communion between two parts of the Anglican Communion mean a Communion-wide split with each province having to choose between one side or the other? How will these divisions affect the relationship of each province with the See of Canterbury as the centre of unity of the Communion?"

In order to answer these questions, Cameron said, the primates requested that the Archbishop of Canterbury establish a Commission "which will report in twelve months time to the next meeting of the Primates. Until then, provinces have been urged by the Primates to avoid precipitate action."

Within two weeks, Williams announced the formation of a new Lambeth Commission on Communion, whose mandate was "to look at life in the Anglican Communion in the light of recent events."[10]

Its members were to be appointed by the Archbishop of Canterbury. Its chair would be Eames, a veteran arbitrator of conflicts between Roman Catholics and Protestants in Northern Ireland, as well as previous intra-Anglican disputes over the ordination of women. The commission was first known informally as "Eames II" — a nod to the "Archbishop of Canterbury's Commission on Communion and Women in the Episcopate" of 1988, chaired by Eames, and its successor organization, known as the Eames Monitoring Group.

According to the Anglican Communion News Service (ACNS), the Commission's "main task would be to offer advice on finding a way through the situation which currently threatens to divide the Communion." Quoting Williams:

> The Primates were clear that the Anglican Communion could be approaching a crucial and critical point in its life. The responses of Provinces to developing events will determine the future life of our Communion in a profound way and we need to take time for careful prayer, reflection and consideration to discern God's will for the whole Communion. This Commission, under the Communion's longest serving Primate, is intended to contribute to our finding a way forward.

"I am conscious of the importance and the delicacy of the work the Commission will have to undertake. It is important to see the whole of the task — we have not been charged with finding the answers to the questions of sexuality, but with assisting the Communion to respond to recent developments in our churches in North America in a way which is fully faithful to Christ's call for the Unity of his Church," the ACNS quoted Eames as responding.[11]

The mandate given to the Commission was clear.[12]
The Archbishop of Canterbury requests the Commission:

1. To examine and report to him by September 30, 2004, in preparation for the ensuing meetings of the Primates and the Anglican Consultative Council, on the legal and theological implications flowing from the decisions of the Episcopal Church (USA) to appoint a priest in a committed same sex relationship as one of its bishops, and of the Diocese of New Westminster to authorise services for use in connection with same sex unions, and specifically on the canonical understandings of communion, impaired and broken communion, and the ways in which provinces of the Anglican Communion may relate to one another in situations where the ecclesiastical authorities of one province feel unable to maintain the fullness of communion with another part of the Anglican Communion.

2. Within their report, to include practical recommendations (including reflection on emerging patterns of provision for episcopal oversight for those Anglicans within a particular jurisdiction, where full communion within a province is under threat) for maintaining the highest degree of communion that may be possible in the circumstances resulting from these decisions, both within and between the churches of the Anglican Communion.

3. Thereafter, as soon as practicable, and with particular reference to the issues raised in Section IV of the Report of the Lambeth Conference 1998, to make recommendations to the Primates and the Anglican Consultative Council, as to the exceptional circumstances and conditions under which, and the means by which, it would be appropriate for the Archbishop of Canterbury to exercise an extraordinary ministry of episcope (pastoral oversight), support and reconciliation with regard to the internal affairs of a province other than his own for the sake of maintaining communion with the said province and between the said province and the rest of the Anglican Communion.

4. In its deliberations, to take due account of the work already undertaken on issues of communion by the Lambeth Conferences of 1988 and 1998, as well as the views expressed by the Primates of the Anglican Communion in the communiqués and pastoral letters arising from their meetings since 2000.

The members of the Commission were drawn from across the far-flung Communion. They consisted of:[13]

- Archbishop Robin Eames, Primate of All Ireland, Chairman
- The Rev. Canon Alyson Barnett-Cowan, Director of Faith, Worship and Ministry for the Anglican Church of Canada
- Bishop David Beetge, Dean of the Church of the Province of Southern Africa
- Professor Norman Doe, Director of the Centre for Law and Religion, Cardiff University, Wales
- Bishop Mark Dyer, Director of Spiritual Formation, Virginia Theological Seminary, USA
- Archbishop Drexel Gomez, Primate of the West Indies
- Archbishop Josiah Iduwo-Fearon, Archbishop of Kaduna, the Anglican Church of Nigeria

- The Rev. Dorothy Lau, Director of the Hong Kong Sheng Kung Hui Welfare Council
- Anne McGavin, Advocate, formerly legal adviser to the College of Bishops of the Scottish Episcopal Church
- Archbishop Bernard Malango, Primate of Central Africa
- Dr. Esther Mombo, Academic Dean of St Paul's United Theological Seminary, Limuru, Kenya
- Archbishop Barry Morgan, Primate of Wales
- Chancellor Rubie Nottage, Chancellor of the West Indies
- Bishop John Paterson, Primate of Aotearoa, New Zealand and Polynesia, and Chairman of the Anglican Consultative Council
- Dr. Jenny Te Paa, Principal of College of Saint John the Evangelist, Auckland, New Zealand
- Bishop James Terom, Moderator, the Church of North India
- Bishop N. Thomas Wright, Bishop of Durham, the Church of England.

Advising the commission were:

- The Rev. Canon John Rees, legal adviser to the Anglican Consultative Council, legal consultant to the commission
- The Rev. Canon Gregory Cameron, director of Ecumenical Affairs and Studies, Anglican Communion Office, secretary to the commission

The fledgling commission scheduled three meetings — one for February at Windsor in England; a June gathering at the Kanuga Conference Center in North Carolina (USA); and a final gathering at Windsor in September 2004 to complete its "initial report on the nature, extent and consequences of Impaired Communion in the Anglican Communion as a result of recent developments" for submission to the Archbishop of Canterbury in October.

Public sessions were not envisioned, but "evidence considered by the Commission" was to be published on the commission's Web site, and interim reports would follow each of the plenary sessions.

The "submissions of evidence" were to address the Commission's eight "key questions":[14]

1. What are (a) the legal and (b) the theological implications flowing from ECUSA decision to appoint a priest in a committed same sex relationship as one of its bishops? (See LC 1998 Res. I.10)

2. What are (a) the legal and (b) the theological implications of the decision of the diocese of New Westminster to authorise services for use in connection with same sex unions?

3. What are the canonical understandings of (a) communion, (b) impaired communion and (c) broken communion? (What is autonomy and how is it related to communion?)

4. How (do and) may provinces relate to one another in situations where the ecclesiastical authorities of one province feel unable to maintain the fullness of communion with another part of the Anglican Communion?

5. What practical solutions might there be to maintain the highest degree of communion that may be possible, in the circumstances resulting from these two decisions, within the individual churches involved? (eg [alternative] episcopal oversight when full communion is threatened)

6. What practical solutions might there be to maintain the highest degree of communion that may be possible, in the circumstances resulting from these two decisions, as between the churches of the Anglican Communion? (eg [alternative] episcopal oversight when full communion is threatened)

7. Under (a) what circumstances, (b) what conditions, and (c) by what means might it be appropriate for the Archbishop of Canterbury to exercise an extraordinary ministry of pastoral oversight, support and reconciliation with regard to the internal affairs of a province to maintain communion between Canterbury and that province? (see LC 1998, Res. IV.13)

8. Under (a) what circumstances, (b) what conditions, and (c) by what means might it be appropriate for the Archbishop of Canterbury to exercise an extraordinary ministry of pastoral oversight, support and reconciliation with regard to the internal affairs of a province to maintain communion between that province and the rest of the Anglican Communion? (see LC 1998, Res. IV.13)

In fact, the commission was being called upon to address a question that had bothered Anglicans — and their ecumenical partners in Christendom — for a long time: How do Anglicans define what is authentically Anglican, and what is not? Who makes the decision? And who makes it stick?

The story told about Anglicans by others usually involves a willful Henry VIII and a questionable divorce and remarriage denied by the Pope. But the story most Anglicans have told about themselves in the last two centuries is one of the catholic Church in the realm of England asserting its ancient rights to practice the apostolic faith in its native cultural context and language without the intervention of a foreign prelate, the Bishop of Rome — in effect, cutting ties with the last representative of the Roman Empire to which Britain and its church had once belonged. And in truth, the English Reformation was different in character from the continental Reformation of Luther and Calvin. Within a half-century of Elizabeth I's religious settlement of 1559, members of the English Church were beginning to stress its continuity with, rather than difference from, an episcopally structured "church catholic," if not the Catholic Church in Rome.

When England became an empire itself, and its commercial, political, and military arms took dominion over lands and peoples in both the Eastern and Western Hemispheres, the Church of England went with them — first to serve the spiritual needs of English people, then to convert the colonized to the Christian faith. As those colonies, beginning with the United States of America, won or were granted their independence, the question of the relationship of England's national church to the churches in its former colonies, now nations in their own right, became critical.

The idea of an "Anglican Communion" eventually emerged as a partial response: a fellowship of national churches, or provinces within national or cultural boundaries, all with common roots in the English national church and the British Empire, held together by vaguely defined "bonds of affection" but not juridical authority. The principle that had guided the English Reformation — the idea that each national church or political community should have the autonomy to guide its own development and en-culturation of the catholic and reformed message without foreign interference — was regarded as foundational.

And it was, so long as the vestiges of Empire kept the former colonies culturally close to Britain, and as long as their bish-ops were largely drawn from British ranks. But the upheavals of the twentieth century made theological and cultural cohesion increasingly difficult for those who now called themselves An-glicans. Globalization, among other pressures, meant that the cultural tectonic plates of America, Australia, Africa, and Asia would crunch uncomfortably against one another with each suc-ceeding Lambeth Conference. The remnants of Victorian English Evangelicalism, a burgeoning American Pentecostalism, and the pressures of resurgent Islam confronted one another in the uncer-tain democracies and nervous dictatorships of the Two Thirds World, while Western nations continued to struggle with the legacy of the Enlightenment, in the disillusionment with easy answers of a post-Holocaust and post-Communist world.[15]

Since the 1978 Lambeth Conference, on the heels of the ordi-nation of women in the United States and other churches, "the boundaries and identity of Anglicanism have never been far from the Communion's agenda," according to the Rev. Philip Thomas of Durham, England, assistant to the chair of the Inter-Anglican Theological and Doctrinal Commission (IATDC), writing in a paper submitted to the Lambeth Commission. Then, the present-ing issue was the ordination of women to the priesthood. Ten years later, it was women in the episcopate. Now the place of sexuality in the life of the church had taken center stage. Yet "successive crises within the Anglican family confirm how little progress has been made over the past 25 years in clarifying ideas of authority within the Communion." The reason, Thomas said, is not far to seek: "In times of dispute, even within the church, most participants are not so much interested in understanding as winning."[16]

The Lambeth Commission began its work with a Rite of Commissioning conducted by the Archbishop of Canterbury and a charge from him that laid out the dilemma it faced.[17]

> The difficult balance in our Communion as it presently exists is between the deep conviction that we should not look for a single executive authority and the equally deep anxiety about the way in which a single local decision can step beyond what the Communion as whole is committed to, and create division, embarrassment and evangelistic difficulties in other churches.... The question is how we hold together the belief that membership in the Church is God's gift, so that communion always pre-exists ordinary human agreement, and the recognition that a Church faithful to the biblical revelation has to exercise discipline and draw boundaries if it is to proclaim the gospel of Jesus and not its own concerns.
>
> You will not be dealing with a problem that is simply about biblical faithfulness versus fashionable relativism. There are profound biblical principles involved in all the points so far mentioned, which may point to different emphases and solutions. You will need to be aware of the danger of those doctrines of the Church which, by isolating one element of the Bible's teaching, produce distortions — a Church of the perfect or the perfectly unanimous on one side, a Church of general human inspiration or liberation on the other. Anglicanism has had to deal with such tensions from its beginnings — and indeed, so has the Church overall. You will be drawing on a variety of historical and theological resources from every age in confronting the contemporary challenge.

Reviewing first the findings of its predecessors — the Eames Commission (1988–93), the Virginia Report (1994–98), and the Inter-Anglican Theological and Doctrinal Commission, formed in 1999 — the commission received presentations from Dr. Mary Tanner, former General Secretary of the Church of England Council for Christian Unity and former moderator of the Faith and Order Commission of the World Council of Churches; Dr. Paul Avis, current General Secretary for the Church of England Council for Christian Unity; Professor Stephen Sykes, chair of the Inter-Anglican Theological and Doctrinal Commission; and Dr. Chris Sugden, director of the Oxford Centre for Mission Studies.

In its first interim report, issued following the February 2004 meeting, the commission reported itself "saddened that tensions within the Communion, exacerbated by the use of strident language, have continued to rise in recent months. In addition, there has been the declaration from significant numbers of Anglican Provinces of impaired or broken communion with the Episcopal Church (USA) and the Diocese of New Westminster, Canada.... The Commission requests all members of the Anglican Communion to refrain from any precipitate action, or legal proceedings, which would further harm 'the bonds of communion' in the period whilst it completes its work."[18]

In April, Archbishop Eames found it necessary to repeat the request for patience.[19]

> First, the Commission needs and I believe deserves space to do its work. Actions and statements however well intentioned which express definitive positions on relationships within the Anglican Communion run the danger of limiting the opportunities and options available to the Commission....
>
> Second, I feel it is important that without prejudice to the Report of the Commission, we maintain the highest possible degrees of communion among those who adopt differing views at this time. In that regard those in North America who feel obliged to object to developments in the General Convention of the Episcopal Church or in the Diocese of New Westminster are still to be regarded as faithful Anglicans or Episcopalians so long as these dissenting groups do not initiate schism in their own Churches. On my visit to the United States I was impressed by those who expressed a desire to remain within ECUSA despite the strength of their feelings. Their initiatives to finding a way of maintaining communion within the Episcopal Church (USA) and the Diocese of New Westminster is further evidence of that desire, but I feel such schemes will only be successful if dissenting groups are afforded sufficient support to feel their place within our Anglican family is secure. I would also hope that the wish of the Primates expressed last October that such schemes would be undertaken in consultation with the Archbishop of Canterbury will be observed.
>
> Third, it is obvious to the Commission that if any groups, either dissenting from the decisions of General Convention in ECUSA, or from the forthcoming decisions of the General Synod in Canada, initiate definitive breaks from their parent church, then a different

situation will arise for our deliberations. The Commission would have to regard such decisions as a serious development. But until the Commission has come up with proposals for the way in which we may handle such divisions together as a Communion, the support or encouragement of other provinces or dioceses would seem to be itself a further damaging of trust and mutual life and of the very clear guidelines concerning jurisdictional boundaries that we have agreed to adopt as a Communion at successive Lambeth Conferences.

The letter struck a nerve with a commission member who had been outspoken against the American and Canadian churches' actions: Archbishop Drexel Gomez of the West Indies, who wrote to Eames in May.[20]

Whilst your letter made some important and valuable points, to which I hope we will all give attention, I felt that the call for restraint appeared to be addressed only to those who take objection to recent developments. Surely, in this grave situation, all sides need to give space for the Commission's work.

There is no small feeling amongst conservative members of the Communion that they are being asked to show restraint whilst the liberal agenda moves ahead, with bishops in ECUSA taking action against conservative parishes; the Church of Canada proceeding to debate the blessing of same sex unions; dioceses in the Episcopal Church actually going forward with the authorisation of such rites, and the appointment of known advocates of same sex unions to senior office in the Church of England. This is only likely to create a situation where the playing field is perceived as skewed — conservative reaction is held back, whilst liberal viewpoints are allowed to claim too much territory. It creates the question in many minds, "Why should we wait, if others are not showing the same restraint?" I should be grateful therefore if some way could be found of addressing this question, and pointing out to our Communion that in the period of preparation of the work of the Lambeth Commission, restraint needs to be shown on all sides, and provocation to "precipitate action" avoided.

Eames replied:

Of course, you are quite right: in asking for the Communion to hold back from precipitate action, the Primates were asking for space for the Commission's work by all sides to this debate. I take very seriously indeed the points you make, and consideration will have to be given to events across the Communion which seem to take further controversial positions on the issue of ministry by and to homosexual persons. It makes it more difficult for conservatives on this issue to hold back from strong reaction if they are faced with what can be seen as continuing provocation.

But he went on to quote his own words to the General Synod in Armagh:

> Fundamental to the current situation is what sort of Anglican Communion do we want?
>
> We are not bound to each other by rigid rules or regulations. We share fundamentals of belief, doctrine and practice. We subscribe to "bonds of affection" with each other rather than seeing the Church of England or Canterbury as some sort of central curia. . . .
>
> Second, we share together in the mission of the Church which is to preach Christ crucified to the world. Sadly I feel the current controversies have the potential to damage that mission by diverting us from our main task. We may well ask — are these the sort of issues we really want to divide us or to weaken our mission to suffering humanity? Where should our priorities lie?
>
> Third, we hold as a priority the centrality of Holy Scripture to our witness, worship and life. The fact that pilgrims on the journey of the Church can differ on the interpretation of that same Scripture has produced much of our present crisis. So we need guidance on how we interpret Scripture.

The second meeting of the commission, held in June 2004 at the Kanuga Conference Center in North Carolina, brought the Episcopal Church's protagonists on both sides in person to confront questions. The commission's laconic press release belied the potential for drama in the encounter between opposites.[21]

> On Tuesday, June 15, the Commission received the Presiding Bishop of the Episcopal Church (USA), the Most Revd Frank Griswold, accompanied by Mr. David Booth Beers, Chancellor of the Episcopal Church USA, Mrs Barbara Braver, Assistant to the Presiding Bishop for Communications, the Rt Revd Charles Jenkins, President of the Presiding Bishop's Council of Advice, the Very Revd George Werner, President of the House of Deputies, and the Rt Revd Arthur Williams, former Vice-President of the House of Bishops, who spoke to the Commission. They also received the Bishop of Pittsburgh, the Rt Revd R Duncan, as Moderator of the

Network of Anglican Communion Dioceses and Parishes, accompanied by Mr Hugo Blankingship, Dr Michael Howell, Mrs Diane Knippers, the Revd Canon Martyn Minns, and Mrs Angela Minns.

In fact, leaders of the Network, while claiming that its formation had been encouraged by the Archbishop of Canterbury, had already declared — through a private document uncovered the previous December by the *Washington Post* — the intention to seek to replace the Episcopal Church as the Canterbury-recognized representative of the Anglican Communion in the United States. Many of the Network's leaders and members were also part of the American Anglican Council (AAC), a conservative lobbying group formed in the late 1990s and maintaining close ties to Knippers's Institute for Religion and Democracy, a think tank dedicated to the "reform" of mainline denominations in a conservative direction. The group soon began styling itself the "Anglican Communion Network," though its corporate name remained the same on its Web site and official documents.[22]

Submissions to the commission by various groups and individuals appeared on the Internet. Initially most of the papers and statements were in opposition to the American and Canadian churches' actions. Most had very little to do with the questions posed by the Commission itself — a dilemma noted by the first notes which tracked submissions up to June 12:[23]

> Of the 105 submissions received to date, relatively few respond directly to the complete set of the Commission's key questions, tending instead to focus on particular issues — some of which do not fall specifically within the Commission's mandate (eg, the morality or immorality of same-sex relationships) but which are noted below. The submissions represent a broad spectrum of theology, opinion and perspective but reveal a significant degree of polarity.

By September, the commission noted, more moderate voices had weighed in.[24]

> Whilst schism was considered inevitable in a significant number of the earlier submissions, a prevalent hope expressed in the more

recent submissions summarised below was that unity could and should be sustained, both within ECUSA and among the Anglican Communion. This hope was not wholly constrained to those accepting the actions of ECUSA and the Anglican Church in Canada but was also expressed by some individuals opposed to these actions and by groups whose membership represents a broad spectrum of views.

Nevertheless, the Anglican world was on edge for most of the year, waiting for the word from Windsor in October — a word that some regarded as a last hope for reconciliation.

Lambeth Commission chair Archbishop Robin Eames set the tone for the Windsor Report, named for the site of two of its meetings, when he began his foreword to the document by posing the question, "What do we believe is the will of God for the Anglican Communion?"[25]

Over the past thirty years, said Eames, controversies over human sexuality have become "increasingly divisive and destructive" in the church. Three events drove the current debate for the Anglican Communion:

- the decision by the 74th General Convention of the Episcopal Church (USA) to ratify the election of Gene Robinson, a priest in a long-term committed same-sex relationship, as Bishop of New Hampshire;

- the authorizing by a diocese of the Anglican Church of Canada of a public Rite of Blessing for same-sex unions; and

- the involvement in other provinces by bishops without the consent or approval of the incumbent bishop to perform episcopal functions.

Division over those actions manifested itself at all levels of Anglican life, as well as "bewilderment" on the part of many at the intensity of others. What made this reaction different from other controversies — particularly, Eames said, the question of the ordination of women to the priesthood and episcopate, which emerged at roughly the same time as questions of human sexuality — was that the "depth of conviction and feeling on all sides of the current issues has on occasions introduced a degree of harshness and a lack of charity which is new to Anglicanism. ... Modern methods of communication and in particular the internet have become powerful means of expressing and influencing opinion" — and not always in helpful ways, said Eames.

In the process of the debate over sexuality, deeper questions were raised about

- the nature of authority in the Anglican Communion,
- the interrelationship of the traditional Instruments of Unity (the Archbishop of Canterbury, the Lambeth Conference, the Anglican Consultative Council, and the Primates Meeting)
- the ways in which Anglicans interpret the Bible;
- the priorities of the historic autonomy enshrined in Anglican provinces, and
- issues of justice.

In spite of strong feelings on all sides of the sexuality issue, the primates opted for the new commission to consider those deeper questions and search for "ways in which communion and understanding could be enhanced where serious differences threatened the life of a diverse worldwide Church."

"This Report is not a judgment. It is part of a process," Eames wrote. "It is part of a pilgrimage towards healing and reconciliation. The proposals which follow attempt to look forward rather than merely to recount how difficulties have arisen."

THE REPORT

The report itself was divided into four sections, with four appendices:[26]

Section A: The Purposes and Benefits of Communion

Section B: Fundamental Principles

Section C: Our Future Life Together

Section D: The Maintenance of Communion

Section A: The Purposes and Benefits of Communion

Section A began by considering the biblical foundations of the idea of Communion. "God has unveiled, in Jesus Christ, his glorious plan for the rescue of the whole created order from all that defaces, corrupts and destroys it," stated the report. Therefore, "God's people are to be, through the work of the Spirit, an anticipatory sign of God's healing and restorative future for the world." Thus, the unity of the church, the communion of all its members, and the radical holiness to which all Christ's people are called are all "rooted in the trinitarian life and purposes of the one God" and signify "a new way of being human" to the world.

Citing the apostle Paul's letters to the Ephesians and Corinthians, the section emphasized that, despite deep differences, the ultimate source of the church's unity is in Christ, not itself, and that its purpose lies in God's rescue mission to the world and not in its own internal concerns.

The report then turned to the "practical consequences of a healthy communion" and the ways in which the Anglican Communion has worked out its mission "up to now."

The foundations of Anglican life in communion were identified as:

- a common pattern of liturgical life "rooted in the tradition of the Books of Common Prayer";

- "continual reading, both corporate and private, of the Holy Scriptures";

- a common history "through the See of Canterbury"; and

- "a web of relationships...that are the means and the signs of common life."

The formal expression of these relationships of communion came at the third "Anglican Congress," held in Toronto in 1963, which adopted the phrase "mutual interdependence and responsibility in the Body of Christ" and a group of ten Principles of Partnership by which the Communion has been guided since.

"When these principles have been lived out and honored, there have been practical consequences which have advanced the mission of the church and enhanced the life of the people of the Communion and of the world it exists to serve," said the report. "...They are signs of a healthy attentiveness to the needs of other parts of the body and, moreover, of respect for the insights, hopes, beliefs and convictions of others within the Communion.... What has been less clear in Anglicanism is exactly how this organic body should be sustained."

The report then briefly recounted the story of ordination of women to the priesthood and episcopate as "a recent example of mutual discernment and decision-making within the Anglican Communion."

What the report called "a period of debate and disagreement" regarding Florence Li Tim-Oi's 1944 ordination to the priesthood was not expanded upon.[27] The report picked up the women's ordination narrative with the request of the Diocese of Hong Kong and Macao to the 1968 Lambeth Conference for a ruling on the ordination of women. Lambeth Resolutions 34 to 38 requested that churches or provinces study the question, and recommended that "before any national or regional church makes a final decision to ordain women to the priesthood the advice of the Anglican Consultative Council should be sought and carefully considered."

According to Bishop Gilbert Baker, who succeeded Hall as Hong Kong's bishop, the resolutions were reported to the Council of the Church of South-East Asia in the following spring. (Of its member churches, Taiwan and the Philippine Episcopal Church were part of the Episcopal Church USA, and the other Anglican dioceses were under the metropolitical authority of Canterbury.) A study was undertaken and the diocesan synod voted in January 1970 in favor of the ordination of women. Baker took the question to the Anglican Consultative Council (ACC) at its first meeting in Limuru, Kenya, in 1971. The ACC advised him — "by a small majority" — that if he were to proceed his action would be acceptable and that the ACC would encourage all provinces of the Communion to continue in communion with Hong Kong. Baker ordained two women to the priesthood later that year and recalled, "No bishop or province or national church said anything about not remaining in communion with our diocese."

The Windsor Report goes on to state: "What needs to be noted is that Hong Kong did not understand itself to be so autonomous that it might proceed without bringing the matter to the Anglican Consultative Council as requested by the Lambeth Conference 1968. Furthermore, action was only taken with the co-operation of the Instruments of Unity."[28]

By the 1978 Lambeth Conference, churches in Hong Kong, Canada, the United States, and New Zealand had all ordained women to the priesthood, and eight other provinces had accepted the ordination of women in principle. The bishops passed Resolution 21, recognizing "the legal right of each Church to make its own decision about the appropriateness of admitting women to Holy Orders" while affirming their "commitment to the preservation of unity within and between all member Churches of the Anglican Communion."

When the Episcopal Church's General Convention in 1985 expressed its intention "not to withhold consent to the election of a bishop on the grounds of gender," then–Presiding Bishop Edmond Browning brought the question to the Primates Meeting in Toronto, Canada. The primates requested that Archbishop John Grindrod of Australia head a committee to prepare a paper for the 1988 Lambeth Conference. What became known as the Grindrod Report counseled restraint but acknowledged that if a province went ahead, "persuaded by compelling doctrinal reasons, by its experience of women in the priesthood and by the demands of mission in its region, and with the overwhelming support of the dioceses, such a step should be offered for reception within the Anglican Communion."

By an overwhelming vote, the 1988 Lambeth bishops insisted "that each province respect the decision and attitudes of other provinces in the ordination or consecration of women to the episcopate, without such respect necessarily indicating acceptance of the principles involved, maintaining the highest possible degree of communion with the provinces which differ." A Commission on Women in the Anglican Episcopate, chaired by Archbishop Eames and known simply as "The Eames Commission," tackled the question and reported to Lambeth 1998.

The Windsor Report summed up:

> Anglicans can understand from this story that decision-making in the Communion on serious and contentious issues has been, and can be, carried out without division, despite a measure of impairment. We need to note that the Instruments of Unity, i.e. the Archbishop of Canterbury, the Lambeth Conference, the Anglican Consultative Council and the Primates' Meeting, were all involved in the decision-making process. Provincial autonomy was framed by Anglican interdependence on matters of deep theological concern to the whole Communion.

But, the report went on to say, such a well-ordered process was not followed by the U.S. and Canadian churches on the "highly sensitive and emotionally charged" issues of human sexuality. That fact "lies at the heart of the problems we currently face," which "come in the wake of various other related debates in the Communion, in relation (for instance) to polygamy and to the remarriage of divorced persons":

- whether or not it is legitimate for the church to bless the committed, exclusive and faithful relationships of same sex couples, and

- whether or not it is appropriate to ordain, and/or consecrate to the episcopate, persons living in a sexual relationship with a partner of the same sex.

"Experimentation" with blessings of same-sex relationships within North America dates back as far as 1973, said the report, pointing out that successive Lambeth Conferences in 1978, 1988, and 1998 discussed matters relating to homosexuality and issued resolutions. The report noted that "there has been some controversy" about the way in which the 1998 resolution, Resolution I.10.6, was arrived at and voted upon, but did not elaborate on the nature of the controversy.[29]

Regardless of such questions, the report said, Lambeth Resolution I.10 has been upheld by two of the four Instruments of Unity, the Primates Meeting and the Archbishop of Canterbury, as "the standard of Anglican teaching on the matter" and "*this Commission has not been asked to continue this conversation, nor comment on or reconsider either the Lambeth Resolution or the Primates' Statement. Further serious Communion-wide discussion of the relevant issues is clearly needed as a matter of urgency, but that is not part of our mandate*" (emphasis in original).

In the meantime, "the overwhelming response from other Christians both inside and outside the Anglican family has been to regard these developments as departures from genuine, apostolic Christian faith," and "reaction has not been confined to statements of disagreement and opposition," but included:

- declarations that a state of either impaired or broken communion now exists between Anglican provinces (calling both ecclesiological legitimacy and constitutional authority into question);

- moves by dissenting parishes and groups to seek episcopal oversight from other dioceses and/or provinces; and

- the exercise of episcopal functions by some bishops and archbishops in parts of the Episcopal Church (USA) and the Anglican Church of Canada and without the consent of the relevant diocesan bishop, in violation of Lambeth resolutions and regulations of the undivided church at Nicaea.

"All these developments have now contributed materially to a tit-for-tat stand-off" in the Anglican Communion.

The report then identified six interacting features of contemporary Anglican life that contributed to the impasse in the Communion: questions of theological development, ecclesiastical procedures, adiaphora, subsidiarity, trust, and authority.

Regarding theological development, the report affirmed the necessity for it — and even for "radical innovation" in the service of missionary needs — but raised the question of how to discern "the line between faithful inculturation and false accommodation to the world's ways of thinking." In the judgment of the Commission, ECUSA and the Diocese of New Westminster failed either to make their theological case for such discernment or to consult "meaningfully" with the Communion as a whole about their actions.

Both also failed, the commission said, to follow the procedures that developed in the Communion in response to the issue of women's ordination. This implied that ECUSA and New Westminster believed the questions at issue involved adiaphora — things about which Christians may differ without endangering unity — while other Anglicans regard the issue as a central matter of core doctrine. Matters involving adiaphora are usually decided at the most local level possible, according to the principle of subsidiarity, and so the disagreement between ECUSA and New Westminster, on the one hand, and the rest of the Communion on, the other, on what constitutes adiaphora led to a bitter dispute over whether their decisions were local in nature or should have been reserved for the Communion-wide level.

Mutual trust and mutual responsibility have been eroded, the commission said, with a resulting increase in polarization and oversimplification of issues. The Communion needs "a common forum for debate, a common table to which we can bring our questions for a proper family discussion."

But, the report said, "all of this can be summed up in a word which, though often misunderstood, denotes an elusive sixth element which might hold the key: authority." Lacking an overarching authority figure such as the Pope and the structural mechanisms of Roman Catholic authority, the Anglican Communion has "always declared that its supreme authority is scripture," but has not clarified how that authority works "on the ground." "Urgent fresh thought and action have become necessary" to bridge the gap between the theory and practice of authority in Anglicanism.

Section B: Fundamental Principles

For the second time in the Windsor Report, the Commission at the beginning of Section B felt it necessary to reiterate — with emphasis — that its mandate did not include comment or recommendations on the theology or ethics of homosexuality.

This section of the report examined:

- the nature of communion with God and one another;
- what binds us together and equips us for God's mission in the world; and
- how diversity produces tension and difficulty.

Double "bonds of affection" link Anglicans to one another: the bonds of children of God in Christ, and the bonds of a shared identity in the history of Anglicanism. "This is a relationship of 'covenantal affection'; that is, our mutual affection is not subject to whim and mood, but involves us in a covenant relation of binding mutual promises, with God in Christ and with one another," said the report. Communion is "God's gift as well as God's command." Provinces and churches sharing that common heritage express their mutual relationships in the form of communion with Canterbury, with each other, and through the idea of being part of the Communion.

Communion is about mutual relationships between churches and between individual Christians, expressed by

- community
- equality
- common life
- sharing

- interdependence
- mutual affection and respect

... subsisting in

- visible unity
- common confession of the apostolic faith
- common belief in scripture and the creeds
- common baptism and shared Eucharist
- a mutually recognized common ministry

... and involving

- practicing a common liturgical tradition
- intending to listen, speak, and act alongside one another in obedience to the gospel

To speak of "impaired," "fractured," or "restricted" communion, or of "degrees" of communion between one church or group of churches and another, commonly means that only some of those characteristics of relationship are apparent, varying according to the degree or nature of the impairment. But any such impairment "could in principle call into question the constitutional position of several member churches of the Anglican Communion," particularly those that "mark out their identity in terms precisely of being in full communion either with Canterbury or with all other churches in communion with Canterbury."

Staying in communion, therefore, "makes demands" — obligations and rights flowing from the truths on which a Christian community rests. They include the "ancient canonical principle that what touches all should be decided by all," and the obligation to "act interdependently, not independently."

There are specific bonds which hold the Anglican Communion together:

- the authority of scripture
- the interpretation of scripture
- the episcopate
- discernment in communion and reception

Scripture has always been recognized as the Church's supreme authority, but the common phrase "the authority of scripture" can be misleading, explained the report, and that may be one cause of the divisions in the Communion. The phrase "must be regarded as a shorthand, and a potentially misleading one at that, for the longer and more complex notion of 'the authority of the triune God, exercised through scripture.' "

> The purpose of scripture is not simply to supply true information, nor just to prescribe in matters of belief and conduct, nor merely to act as a court of appeal, but to be part of the dynamic life of the Spirit through which God the Father is making the victory which was won by Jesus' death and resurrection operative within the world and in and through human beings. . . . This, rather than a quasi-legal process of "appeal," is the primary and dynamic context within which the shorthand phrase "authority of scripture" finds its deepest meaning.

As a result, it is essential that Scripture be at the heart of worship and that Christian leaders, particularly bishops, see themselves and are seen primarily as teachers of Scripture. Interpretation of Scripture is "a way of ensuring that it really is scripture that is being heard, not simply the echo of our own voices . . . or the memory of earlier Christian interpretations" — culturally entrenched views, whether "the assumptions and entrenched views of the Enlightenment (which have often resulted in unwarranted negative judgments on much biblical material), as well as . . . the assumptions and entrenched views of a pre- or anti-critical conservatism." Christian scholars cannot claim "a detached neutrality" with regard to biblical interpretation; they must be able to explain how an alternate view builds up the church, and the church must be prepared to listen, test, and even change its mind if the case is made.

"The current crisis thus constitutes a call to the whole Anglican Communion to re-evaluate the ways in which we have read, heard, studied and digested scripture," said the report. "If our present difficulties force us to read and learn together from scripture in new ways, they will not have been without profit."

Another element holding the Communion together is the "threefold order of ministry, in continuity with the early Church." Bishops "represent the universal Church to the local and vice versa," and therefore, as powerful symbols of unity between churches, "attention to [the] general acceptability" of a bishop across the wider church is essential to keep the episcopate from becoming "an occasion and focus of disunity" instead.

"What this bears witness to is the understanding that the churches of the Anglican Communion, if that Communion is to mean anything at all, are obliged to move together, to walk together in synodality," the report went on. "It is by listening to, and interacting with, voices from as many different parts of the family as possible that the Church discovers what its unity and communion really mean."

Churches and individuals also must learn to discern Scripture in communion in order to avoid a culturally biased reading. "...One of the ways in which we discern the limits of appropriate inculturation is by our rendering account to one another, across traditional boundaries, for the gospel we proclaim and live and the teaching we offer." Fresh developments need to be submitted to the test of reception across the Communion, with the *consensus fidelium* (common mind of the believers) as "the ultimate check that a new declaration was in harmony with the faith as it had been received." The commission saw this as a threefold sequence of theological debate and discussion, formal action, and increased consultation "to see whether the formal action settles down and makes itself at home."

The report cautioned, however, that not every development should be subject to the doctrine of reception. "It cannot be applied in the case of actions which are explicitly against the current teaching of the Anglican Communion as a whole, and/or of individual provinces. No province, diocese or parish has the right to introduce a novelty which goes against such teaching and excuse it on the grounds that it has simply been put forward for reception."

Unity in the Anglican Communion includes the diversity that comes from factors such as local culture and different traditions of reading Scripture, and this diversity is enshrined in the autonomy of the individual provinces, something that is "fundamental to Anglican polity" and yet also poses the risk of "great tension and division."

The report briefly traced the development of Anglican understandings of provincial autonomy, from the sixteenth-century break with Rome to the more recent concept of "independence from the control of the British Crown" and "the right of each church to self-determination" over local issues. But Anglican autonomy is closer to the orthodox idea of "autocephaly" — of autonomy in communion — than to the notion of autonomy as sovereignty or independence; "not an isolated individualism, but the idea of being free to determine one's own life within a wider obligation to others."

Linked to subsidiarity, autonomy "denotes not unlimited freedom but what we might call freedom-in-relation, so it is subject to limits generated by the commitments of communion."

In matters of common concern, churches should (subject to discernment with the Instruments of Unity):

- consider, promote and respect the common good of the Anglican Communion and its constituent churches;

- maintain communion with fellow churches by bringing potentially contentious initiatives to the rest of the communion;

- be able to depart, where appropriate and acceptable, on the basis of its own corporate conscience and with the blessing of the communion, from the standards of the community of which it is an autonomous part, provided such departure is neither critical to the maintenance of communion nor likely to harm the common good of the Anglican Communion and of the Church universal.

The limits to diversity in the life of Christian churches are defined by truth and charity.

The idea of adiaphora, those "things which do not make a difference" about which the church can disagree without dividing, has been "a major feature of Anglican theology, over against those schools of thought, both Roman and Protestant, in which even the smallest details of belief and practice are sometimes regarded as essential parts of an indivisible whole." But despite the ideas of current postmodern discourse, "not all 'differences' can be tolerated" in the church. Certain principles help the church decide which behaviors are adiaphora and which are not. "That which embodies and expresses renewed humanity in Christ is always mandatory for Christians; that which embodies the dehumanizing turning-away-from-God which Paul characterizes with such terms as 'sin,' 'flesh,' and so on, is always forbidden." Yet "even when the notion of *'adiaphora'* applies, it does not mean that Christians are left free to pursue their own personal choices without restriction."

Each claim of adiaphora should be subject to two questions:

- is this in fact the kind of matter which can count as "inessential," or does it touch on something vital?
- is it something that, nevertheless, a sufficient number of other Christians will find scandalous and offensive?

"...If the answer to the latter question is 'yes,' the biblical guidelines insist that those who have no scruples about the proposed action should nevertheless refrain from going ahead."

"Adiaphora" and "subsidiarity" work together like this:

- the clearer it is that something is "indifferent" in terms of the Church's central doctrine and ethics, the closer to the local level it can be decided;
- whereas the clearer it is that something is central, the wider must be the circle of consultation.

But this poses the question of how does one know, and who decides, where a particular issue belongs? And that, said the report, leads back to the role of the Anglican Communion's Instruments of Unity.

Section C: Our Future Life Together

The Instruments of Unity refers (in historical order) to:

- The Archbishop of Canterbury
- The Lambeth Conference
- The Anglican Consultative Council
- The Primates Meeting

For Anglicans, the Archbishop of Canterbury — person and office — was and is "the pivotal instrument and focus of unity . . . a touchstone of what it was to be Anglican." Flowing naturally from this was the idea that the Archbishop of Canterbury would call the bishops of the Anglican Communion together for counsel in the Lambeth Conference — not a "pan-Anglican Synod, with legislative powers, but rather as an advisory body," the expression of the collegiality of Anglican bishops.

With the increased awareness of lay participation in formal synodical government, the idea of an Anglican Consultative Council (ACC) emerged, designed to give a voice to laypeople in the Communion — though the ACC, like the Lambeth Conference, "has always disavowed any intention to develop a more formal synodical status." (At the 2002 ACC meeting in Hong Kong, a resolution was passed asking the Archbishop of Canterbury to "explore the possibility of a more representative gathering" by inviting clergy and laypeople to the Lambeth Conferences.)

The youngest of the Instruments of Unity is the Primates Meeting, initiated in 1978 as a consultative and advisory authority — though that may change, since "in part, it is the task of the present Commission to consider proposals . . . for the Primates to have an 'enhanced responsibility in offering guidance on doctrinal, moral and pastoral matters.' "

The commission then moved into its recommendations on the status of the Instruments of Unity. Not favored was "the accumulation of formal power by the Instruments of Unity, or the establishment of any kind of central 'curia' for the Communion." Rather, the commission wanted the Archbishop of Canterbury to be the "focus of unity" and the Primates Meeting, Lambeth Conference, Anglican Consultative Council, and "possibly others," to be regarded as the "Instruments of Communion." Yet to be worked out was the relationship between the instruments, particularly between the Lambeth Conference and the Anglican Consultative Council.

Strengthening the role of the Archbishop of Canterbury was a trend the commission wanted to encourage; he "must not be regarded as a figurehead, but as the central focus of both unity and mission" in the Communion and the person who can "articulate the mind of the Communion especially in areas of controversy" without being regarded as an "outside interference" in the affairs of any province. The Archbishop should have total discretion, the commission said, with respect to invitations to the Lambeth Conference and to the Primates Meeting.

Mindful that the Archbishop of Canterbury is the only individual of the four Instruments of Communion, the commission "concludes that the establishment of a Council of Advice would considerably enhance the foundations of any authority on which the Archbishop might feel truly enabled to act. In addition, the relationship between the Archbishop and the Secretariat of the Anglican Consultative Council must be reconsidered." A new council could be drawn from such bodies as the Joint Standing Committees of the Anglican Consultative Council and the Primates Meeting.

In recent years the idea of an Anglican "common law" between provinces gained currency, and the Windsor Report expressed a desire to explore the idea of shared principles of canon law — a *ius commune* — as a "fifth instrument of unity." In addition to asking the Anglican Communion Legal Advisers' Network to produce a simple and short domestic "communion law," one of the innovations of the Windsor Report was the idea of a common Anglican covenant, similar to the concordats and other ecumenical agreements signed by individual provinces with churches outside the Communion and incorporated into the legal systems of Anglican churches and provinces.

Such a covenant, though it would have "no binding authority," would deal with

- the acknowledgment of common identity
- the relationships of communion
- the commitments of communion
- the exercise of autonomy in communion
- the management of communion affairs (including disputes)

The commission suggested the covenant be subjected to a process consisting of:

- discussion and approval of a first draft by the Primates
- submission to the member churches and the Anglican Consultative Council
- final approval by the Primates
- legal authorization by each church for signing
- a solemn signing by the Primates in a liturgical context.

The Commission believed that "the case for adoption of an Anglican Covenant is overwhelming":

- The Communion cannot afford repeated worldwide inter-Anglican conflict.
- The concept of the adoption of a covenant is not new in the ecumenical context.
- Adoption of a covenant is a practical need and a theological challenge.
- The act of entering a covenant carries the weight of international obligation.
- A covenant may assist churches in their relations with the States in which they exist.
- Some provisions will be susceptible to development.

Section D: The Maintenance of Communion

The Commission "regrets that without attaching sufficient importance to the interests of the wider Communion":

- The Episcopal Church (USA) proceeded with the consecration of Gene Robinson
- The 74th General Convention declared that "local faith communities are operating within the bounds of our common life as they explore and experience liturgies celebrating and blessing same-sex unions"
- The Diocese of New Westminster approved the use of public Rites for the Blessing of same sex unions

- The General Synod of the Anglican Church of Canada issued a statement affirming the integrity and sanctity of committed same sex relationships

- A number of primates and other bishops have taken it upon themselves to intervene in the affairs of other provinces of the Communion.

The commission's unanimous recommendations follow.

Since bishops "represent the universal to the local, and the local to the universal," and the communion has expressed its mind negatively on same-gender unions, the election and confirmation of Gene Robinson "caused deep offence to many faithful Anglican Christians," and therefore those involved in the process of his election "should in future in the light of all that has happened pay proper regard to the acceptability of the candidate to other provinces in our Communion."

The commission recommended that:

- "...The Episcopal Church (USA) be invited to express its regret that the proper constraints of the bonds of affection were breached...and for the consequences which followed, and that such an expression of regret would represent the desire of the Episcopal Church (USA) to remain within the Communion."

- Those who took part as consecrators of Gene Robinson should be "invited to consider" whether they should withdraw themselves from representative functions in the Anglican Communion.

- "...The Episcopal Church (USA) be invited to effect a moratorium on the election and consent to the consecration of any candidate to the episcopate who is living in a same gender union until some new consensus in the Anglican Communion emerges."

- "...The Instruments of Unity, through the Joint Standing Committee, find practical ways in which the 'listening' process commended by the Lambeth Conference in 1998 may be taken forward ...on the underlying issue of same gender relationships."

The commission also requested that the Episcopal Church (USA) explain with reference to Scripture, tradition, and reason "how a person living in a same gender union may be considered eligible to lead the flock of Christ."

On the public blessing of same-sex unions, the commission called for a moratorium and recommended that U.S. and Canadian bishops who have authorized such rites "be invited to express regret that the proper constraints of the bonds of affection were breached by such authorization" and "be invited to consider in all conscience whether they should withdraw themselves from representative functions in the Anglican Communion."

The commission commended "Caring for all the Churches," the proposal for delegated episcopal pastoral oversight (DEPO) set out by the House of Bishops of the Episcopal Church (USA) in 2004, rather than "the establishment of parallel jurisdictions." Those bishops who have refused to utilize DEPO with dissenting congregations were urged to "reconsider" their position.

Bishops who believe it is their "conscientious duty" to intervene in other provinces, dioceses, and parishes were invited to express regret for the consequences of their actions, affirm their desire to remain in the Communion, effect a moratorium on any further interventions, and seek an accommodation with the bishops of the dioceses whose parishes they have taken into their own care. All parties to the current dispute were urged "to seek ways of reconciliation, and to heal our divisions."

The final section of the report sounded a somber note. "There remains a very real danger that we will not choose to walk together," it says. "Should the call to halt and find ways of continuing in our present communion not be heeded, then we shall have to begin to learn to walk apart. We would much rather not speculate on actions that might need to be taken if, after acceptance by the Primates, our recommendations are not implemented."

However, they noted, some of the courses that may be followed include:

- processes of mediation and arbitration
- non-invitation to relevant representative bodies and meetings
- invitation, but to observer status only
- as an absolute last resort, withdrawal from membership

The Response

Official responses to the Windsor Report began within hours of its first posting to the Internet on October 18, 2004.

From the Archbishop of Canterbury came a request that "everyone with the well being of our Communion at heart will now take time to study the report — and to pray and reflect upon its proposals which, as the Commission has made clear, offer neither easy nor simple solutions to real and demanding challenges. . . . There is plenty to digest and there should be no rush to judgement."[30]

Members of the commission issued their own statements. Archbishop Bernard Malango, Primate of Central Africa, warned that

> for me, the very last paragraph of the report is important. It clearly sets out the fact that as a commission we have aimed to work for healing and restoration, but it also recognises that there remains the danger that our brothers and sisters may still choose to walk apart. If the recommendations of our report are not taken seriously, then the question of our future together in the Anglican Communion will remain, and greater division may result.[31]

Archbishop Barry Morgan of Wales joined in the note of warning:

> The report needs to be pondered long and hard by the provinces of the Communion and its implications studied before reacting in any precipitate way. The subtleties of the report may not be noticed on first reading. However, if the way forward advocated by this report is found unacceptable then the future for the Anglican Communion is indeed bleak.[32]

Presiding Bishop Frank Griswold of the Episcopal Church (USA) offered his "preliminary observations," beginning with the admonition that the report should "be read carefully as a whole and viewed in its entirety rather than being read selectively to buttress any particular perspectives."[33]

> My first reading shows the Report as having in mind the containment of differences in the service of reconciliation. However, unless we go beyond containment and move to some deeper place of acknowledging and making room for the differences that will doubtless continue to be present in our Communion, we will do disservice to our mission. A life of communion is not for the benefit of the church but for the sake of the world.

But Griswold would not back away from lesbian and gay Episcopalians:

> Given the emphasis of the Report on difficulties presented by our differing understandings of homosexuality, as Presiding Bishop I am obliged to affirm the presence and positive contribution of gay and lesbian persons to every aspect of the life of our church and in all orders of ministry. Other Provinces are also blessed by the lives and ministry of homosexual persons. I regret that there are places within our Communion where it is unsafe for them to speak out of the truth of who they are.
>
> The Report will be received and interpreted within the Provinces of the Communion in different ways, depending on our understanding of the nature and appropriate expression of sexuality. It is important to note here that in the Episcopal Church we are seeking to live the gospel in a society where homosexuality is openly discussed and increasingly acknowledged in all areas of our public life.
>
> For at least the last 30 years our church has been listening to the experience and reflecting upon the witness of homosexual persons in our congregations. There are those among us who perceive the fruit of the Spirit deeply present in the lives of gay and lesbian Christians, both within the church and in their relationships. However, other equally faithful persons among us regard same gender relationships as contrary to scripture. Consequently, we continue to struggle with questions regarding sexuality.
>
> Here I note the Report recommends that practical ways be found for the listening process commended by the Lambeth Conference in 1998 to be taken forward with a view to greater understanding about homosexuality and same gender relationships. It also requests the Episcopal Church to contribute to the ongoing discussion. I welcome this invitation and know that we stand ready to make a contribution to the continuing conversation

and discernment of the place and ministry of homosexual persons in the life of the church.

Griswold affirmed the importance of the "diverse center" of the church — a familiar theme for him:

> The Report calls our Communion to reconciliation, which does not mean the reduction of differences to a single point of view. In fact, it is my experience that the fundamental reality of the Episcopal Church is the diverse center, in which a common commitment to Jesus Christ and a sense of mission in his name to a broken and hurting world override varying opinions on any number of issues, including homosexuality. The diverse center is characterized by a spirit of mutual respect and affection rather than hostility and suspicion. I would therefore hope that some of the ways in which we have learned to recognize Christ in one another, in spite of strongly held divergent opinions, can be of use in other parts of our Communion.
>
> As Presiding Bishop I know I speak for members of our church in saying how highly we value our Communion and the bonds of affection we share. Therefore, we regret how difficult and painful actions of our church have been in many provinces of our Communion, and the negative repercussions that have been felt by brother and sister Anglicans.

But the idea of an overarching Anglican Covenant received a cool reception from Griswold.

> ...One section of the Report recommends the development of a covenant to be entered into by the provinces of the Communion. This notion will need to be studied with particular care. As we and other provinces explore the idea of a covenant we must do so knowing that over the centuries Anglican comprehensiveness has given us the ability to include those who wish to see boundaries clearly and closely drawn and those who value boundaries that are broad and permeable. Throughout our history we have managed to live with the tension between a need for clear boundaries and for room in order that the Spirit might express itself in fresh ways in a variety of contexts.
>
> The Report makes demands on all of us, regardless of where we may stand, and is grounded in a theology of reconciliation and an understanding of communion as the gift of the triune God. It is therefore an invitation for all of us to take seriously the place

in which we presently find ourselves but to do so with a view to a future yet to be revealed.

Archbishop Andrew Hutchison of Canada issued a terse statement that pointed out the significance of the unanimity of the Lambeth Commission "in spite of the cultural and theological differences of its members."

> This indicates that there is a positive will to maintain the unity of the diverse Anglican Communion. The fact that Commission members can speak with one voice holds open the door of hope that our Church can, with prayer and dialogue, persevere in seeking unity.
>
> It is now incumbent upon us, the Canadian Church, as it is for all provinces of the Anglican Communion to study the document and its recommendations. In keeping with the nature of the Anglican Communion, each province is entitled to respond with its own voice and from its own cultural and theological context. We look forward to hearing responses from all Anglican provinces.[34]

Archbishop Njongonkulu Ndungane of Cape Town, South Africa, said that he was

> particularly struck by the emphasis that has been given to the delicate relationship we must sustain between autonomy and interdependence. As the report says, "Communion is, in fact, all about mutual relationship." ... Can we live and work and order our world like this? Granting everyone equal status, equal opportunity? With give and take? Prepared to share together, equitably, honestly and vulnerably? Living reciprocally rather than hierarchically? Conscious of being bound in a single shared humanity, in which, if one suffers, all suffer?[35]

Another African, Archbishop Peter Akinola, the Primate of All Nigeria, was not at all pleased by the report, and said so in no uncertain terms.[36]

> After an initial reading it is clear to me that the report falls far short of the prescription needed for this current crisis. It fails to confront the reality that a small, economically privileged group of people has sought to subvert the Christian faith and impose their new and false doctrine on the wider community of faithful believers. We have watched in sadness as sisters and brothers who have sought to maintain their allegiance to the "faith once delivered to the

saints" have been marginalized and persecuted for their faith. We have been filled with grief as we have witnessed the decline of the North American Church that was once filled with missionary zeal and yet now seems determined to bury itself in a deadly embrace with the spirit of the age. Instead of a clear call for repentance we have been offered warm words of sentimentality for those who have shown no godly sorrow for their actions and harsh words of condemnation for those who have reached out a helping hand to friends in need of pastoral and spiritual care.

The inclusion of boundary-hopping conservative bishops in the report's listing of offenses against unity was particularly galling to Akinola.

Why, throughout the document, is there such a marked contrast between the language used against those who are subverting the faith and that used against those of us, from the Global South, who are trying to bring the church back to the Bible? Where are the expressions of deep concern for the men and women whose witness is jeopardized and whose lives are at risk because of the actions of ECUSA [Episcopal Church of the United States of America]? Where are the words of "deep regret" for the impact of ECUSA's actions upon the Global South and our missionary efforts? Where is the language of rebuke for those who are promoting sexual sins as holy and acceptable behaviour? The imbalance is bewildering. It is wrong to use equal language for unequal actions.

And the Lambeth Commission's refusal to condemn homosexuality also rankled.

The report correctly notes that the Episcopal Church and the Diocese of New Westminster have pushed the Anglican Communion to the breaking point. It rightly states that they did not listen to the clear voices of the Communion and rejected the counsel of all four Instruments of Unity. Therefore it is surprising that the primary recommendation of the report is "greater sensitivity" instead of heartfelt repentance. Already the Presiding Bishop of ECUSA has stated that he sees no need to halt welcoming practising homosexuals into all orders of ministry! In addition, the bishop of New Westminster has indicated that same sex blessing will continue. Thus they are hell bent on destroying the fabric of our common life and we are told to sit and wait.

We have been asked to express regret for our actions and "affirm our desire to remain in the Communion." How patronizing!

We will not be intimidated. In the absence of any signs of repentance and reform from those who have torn the fabric of our
Communion, and while there is continuing oppression of those
who uphold the Faith, we cannot forsake our duty to provide care
and protection for those who cry out for our help.

The Bible says that two cannot walk together unless they are
agreed. The report rightly observes that if the "call to halt" is
ignored "then we shall have to begin to learn to walk apart." The
Episcopal Church and Diocese of New Westminster are already
walking alone on this and if they do not repent and return to the
fold, they will find that they are all alone. They will have broken
the Anglican Communion.

The Provincial Synod of the Southern Cone, announcing its
"full support" for its conservative primate, the Most Rev. Gregory Venables, expressed worry that

> the report has not made a clearer call to repentance on the part
> of the Episcopal Church of the United States and the Anglican
> Church of Canada. They are the ones that have clearly taken de-
> cisions and endorsed practices against the Holy Scriptures and the
> apostolic tradition of two thousand years of ethical teaching of
> the Church and against the clear voice of the Communion. This
> synod insists on what our bishops said in their pastoral letter of
> February 2004, that our relationship with these provinces "can
> only be restored through repentance, pardon and love."[37]

Bishops of the Anglican Church in Aotearoa/New Zealand
and Polynesia issued a pastoral letter deploring the fact that the
Windsor Report

> reached the media before the Church it was written for had read
> it. The debate triggered on the Internet before and after the re-
> port's release bears little resemblance to the careful and prayerful
> process of reception that the Commission proposes....Much of
> the media debate has little to do with what the Windsor Report is
> really about — Which is the question of how we stay together as
> churches within the Anglican Communion and how we keep talk-
> ing to each other across significant divisions of culture, history,
> and understanding of Scripture.[38]

"There is much in this report which is challenging, but it points
us in a sound direction for the resolution of current tensions,"

said the Anglican Primates' Standing Committee, which began its meeting in London just as the report was released.

> It is an invitation to the entire Communion to reflect on our life together. We are conscious of the concerns of those groups whose expectations have not been met, but we are very encouraged by the broad welcome and support that the report has received from many throughout the Communion. As the Primates' Standing Committee it is now our task to put into place the best possible preparations for a considered discussion of the Windsor Report at the meeting of the Primates in Northern Ireland in February 2005.[39]

The Archbishop of Canterbury and the Primates' Standing Committee established a "Reception Reference Group," chaired by the Most Rev. Peter Kwong, Primate of Hong Kong, to receive and coordinate Anglican responses to the Windsor Report.[40] The group consisted of:

- Archbishop Peter Kwong, Primate, Hong Kong, Chair
- Archdeacon Jim Boyles, Provincial Secretary, Canada
- Bishop John Gladstone, Bishop of South Kerala, South India
- Dr. Ishmael Noko, General Secretary, Lutheran World Federation
- Bishop Kenneth Price, Bishop Suffragan of Southern Ohio, USA
- Bishop James Tengatenga, Bishop of Southern Malawi
- Bishop Tito Zavala, Bishop of Chile.

Its staff consultants included:

- The Rev. Canon Gregory Cameron, Anglican Communion Office, secretary
- The Rev. Canon John Rees, Anglican Consultative Council, legal adviser
- The Rev. Sarah Rowland Jones, Church of the Province of Southern Africa.

A set of ten questions developed for the primates and provinces, as well as those for ecumenical partners, were posted on the

Commission's Web site to guide responses to the Windsor Report.

1. How can the 44 churches of the Anglican Communion be helped to stay together?

2. How should a Christian behave when another Christian does something which they believe is deeply offensive to the Gospel?

3. Would you like to see Anglican/Episcopal churches moving closer together or going their separate ways?

Questions posed by the Primates' Standing Committee to the provinces were:

1. What in the description of the life of the Communion in Sections A & B can you recognise as consistent, or not, with your understanding of the Anglican Communion?

2. In which ways do the proposals in Section C & D flow appropriately from the description of the Communion's life in Sections A & B?

3. What do you think are the ways in which the recommendations and proposals of the report would impact on the life of the Communion if they were to be implemented?

4. How would you evaluate the arguments for an Anglican Covenant set out in paragraph 119 of the report? How far do the elements included in the possible draft for such a covenant in Appendix Two of the report represent an appropriate development of the existing life of the Anglican Communion?

Questions to ecumenical partners were:

1. What do you find helpful in the Windsor Report 2004?

2. What questions does the report raise from the perspective of your church?

3. If the recommendations of the Windsor Report were implemented, how would this affect your church's relationship with the Anglican Communion as an ecumenical partner?

The group received a total of 322 responses: 108 from what were referred to as "sectors" — "provinces, dioceses, organizations, Houses of Bishops, theological institutes and mission agencies, as well as the ACC networks and agencies"; 214 were ᶜrom individuals, with 140 from the United States and Canada.

Only thirty originated from Anglicans elsewhere; the rest were from non-Anglicans.

As with the Lambeth Commission itself, some respondents appeared to ignore the Reception Reference Group's questions about the Windsor Report in favor of issuing polemics, pro and con, about homosexuality.

"A minority of these responses directed themselves specifically to the guidelines posed by Archbishop Peter Kwong and those mainly from the sectors," said Scottish Primus Bruce Cameron in presenting the responses to the Primates Meeting, held February 20–25, 2005, at the Dromantine Conference Center in Northern Ireland. "Others... did either an in depth analysis of the Report or responded to the specific issue of the church's attitude to homosexuality."[41]

One significant finding of the group was that, although the controversy was sometimes cast in the media as a liberal/modernist challenge or even dismissal of the authority of Scripture, apparently not a single respondent on either side questioned Scripture's authority per se. But there was "significant disagreement over the question of interpretation of Scripture and the weight we gave to Scripture over against the other Anglican 'authorities' of tradition and reason," and on other issues of authority as well — determining which issues were adiaphora and which were "Communion issues" of concern to all the provinces; who should appoint a Council of Advice for the Archbishop of Canterbury; who would determine the acceptability of any bishop to the entire Communion. "Who decides and how" was a question the commission had not yet answered to the satisfaction of all parties.

Where the Windsor Report had called for "expressions of regret" by the U.S. and Canadian churches, the group noted

> ... different understandings as to what the regret or repentance is for. Is it about the consequences of hurt and pain felt by other parts of the Anglican Communion — the "bonds of affection"? Is it for ignoring the views expressed through the Instruments of Unity — the Lambeth Conference/Primates' Meeting? Or is it that

the acceptance of homosexuality, and expressions of that, is for some ultimately and undeniably wrong in the sight of God?

How a particular respondent understood Windsor's call for regret apparently determined whether or not they felt either of the North American churches had yet adequately answered the call — and, as a result, whether representatives from those churches should withdraw from Anglican gatherings.

Implementing a long-promised "listening process" in conjunction with a time-limited moratorium on the election of bishops unacceptable to the whole Communion and the blessing of same-gender relationships seemed agreeable to most respondents. But there was no overarching agreement on what should be discussed, with whom, and who would foot the bill.

The use of a "language of persecution and victimization" on the part of conservatives as well as gays and lesbians was one factor in the group's raising the question of whether the issue of alternative oversight for dissenting groups had been excessively "personalized." A strong "congregationalist" tone to some of the comments about the need for alternative oversight was noted, as well as a certain amount of overheated rhetoric. Demanding a "reversal" of the U.S. and Canadian decisions, one submission declared that otherwise "we must amputate, to avoid the whole body becoming infected . . . they must be excluded from membership." Another, defending the North American actions, opined that "homosexuals are among those on the cross today."[42]

In their communiqué, written even before the meeting was finished, the primates affirmed the "general thrust" of the Windsor Report but raised "serious questions" about the proposal for an Anglican Covenant, and said they were "cautious of any development which would seem to imply the creation of an international jurisdiction which could override our proper provincial autonomy."[43]

To "restore the full trust of our bonds of affection across the Communion," the primates requested that the two North

American churches "voluntarily withdraw their members from the Anglican Consultative Council (ACC) for the period leading up to the next Lambeth Conference" in 2008, and that both "respond through their relevant constitutional bodies to the questions specifically addressed to them in the Windsor Report as they consider their place within the Anglican Communion." They requested that the ACC organize a hearing at its next meeting so that the North Americans could "set out the thinking behind the recent actions of their Provinces," and also asked the ACC to "take positive steps to initiate the listening and study process which has been the subject of resolutions not only at the Lambeth Conference in 1998, but in earlier Conferences as well." In the meantime, they agreed to "persuade their brothers and sisters to exercise a moratorium on public Rites of Blessing for Same-Sex Unions and on the consecration of any bishop living in a sexual relationship outside Christian marriage."

The communiqué recommended that the Archbishop of Canterbury appoint, "as a matter of urgency, a panel of reference to supervise the adequacy of pastoral provisions" made for dissenting congregations, and committed the primates "neither to encourage nor to initiate cross-boundary interventions" in the internal affairs of other provinces.

But in the days immediately following the meeting, it became apparent that not all the primates were reading off the same page of the communiqué they had just signed. Official reports of the meeting stressed what Williams called "a powerful will" to stay together as a Communion.[44] Unofficial reports were less reassuring. Partisan commentators painted a picture of a communion already fractured — at least in the Eucharistic sense — with conservative primates from the Global South refusing to share in the sacrament in the presence of the North Americans, but being feted at a dinner given after the meeting by American conservatives.[45] Archbishop Gregory Venables of the Southern Cone flew from Dromantine to a meeting of dissident Canadian Anglicans in New Westminster, explaining later that in his view the visit "was not a new initiative" even if the timing "wasn't brilliant."[46]

Reporter Stephen Bates of the U.K.-based *Guardian* wrote that an anonymous primate "not normally noted as a liberal" complained to him that some of the primates were "personally offensive towards Rowan and gratuitously rude about him behind his back. They had no respect for him and said: 'He'll do what we tell him to. . . .' I understand they have been told that American fundamentalist millionaires have promised to match any funding the African church would have received from the Episcopal Church dollar for dollar."[47] Venables, interviewed in the *Church Times,* heatedly denied any rudeness towards Williams and challenged the anonymous primate to come forward.[48]

Meanwhile the Anglican Consultative Council's U.S. and Canadian members struggled with the request by the primates for their withdrawal from the ACC's June 2005 meeting — a request that raised questions about the proper scope of the primates' authority and of the ACC's, as well as new concerns that the voices of Anglican women and laity were being drowned out by the overwhelming preponderance of men and clergy — especially bishops — among the four Instruments of Unity.

CODA

Shortly after the Primates Meeting adjourned, a presentation made by then-Bishop of Monmouth (Wales) Rowan Williams to the 1998 Lambeth Conference appeared on the official Anglican Communion Web site's page for Lambeth Commission–related documents.[49] It was the text of a plenary on making moral decisions, and Williams's conclusions seemed poignantly prescient in light of the events that were to overtake him and the Anglican Communion.

"Local Christian communities gradually and subtly come to take for granted slightly different things, to speak of God with a marked local accent," Williams explained to the Lambeth bishops. " . . . At first sight, when you encounter a different 'accent,' it can sound as though the whole of your Christian world is under attack or at least under question, precisely because no-one learns their Christianity without a local accent." But, he went on,

> . . . what we are looking for in each other is the grammar of obedience: we watch to see if our partners take the same kind of time, sense that they are under the same sort of judgement or scrutiny, approach the issue with the same attempt to be dispossessed by the truth they are engaging with. This will not guarantee agreement; but it might explain why we should always first be hesitant and attentive to each other.
>
> So long as we still have a language in common and the "grammar of obedience" in common, we have, I believe, to turn away from the temptation to seek the purity and assurance of a community speaking with only one voice and to embrace the reality of living in a communion that is fallible and divided. The communion's need for health and mercy is inseparable from my own need for health and mercy. To remain in communion is to remain in solidarity with those who I believe are wounded as well as wounding the Church, in the trust that in the Body of Christ the confronting of wounds is part of opening ourselves to healing.

NOTES

1. "intervene in the pastoral emergency":
   www.aplacetostand.org/dspnews.cfm?id=49;
   www.aplacetostand.org/dspnews.cfm?id=51;
   www.aplacetostand.org/dspnews.cfm?id=74

2. "profoundly aware":
   www.episcopalchurch.org/3577_18343_ENG_HTM.htm

3. Statement:
   www.archbishopofcanterbury.org/releases/2003/030806.html

4. Statement:
   www.archbishopofcanterbury.org/releases/2003/030808.html

5. "September 2003 editorial":
   www.gazette.ireland.anglican.org/260903/focus260903.htm

6. "leisurely thought":
   www.aco.org/primates/index.cfm

7. Statement:
   www.anglicancommunion.org/acns/articles/36/25/acns3633.html

8. News release:
   www.anglicancommunion.org/acns/articles/36/25/acns3635.html

9. "impaired":
   www.anglicancommunion.org/acns/archive/1988/1988-1.htm

10. Statement:
    www.anglicancommunion.org/acns/articles/36slash50/acns3652.html

11. Statement:
    www.anglicancommunion.org/acns/articles/36/50/acns3653.html

12. Statement: "mandate":
    www.anglicancommunion.org/commission/content/mandate.cfm

13. "members":
    www.anglicancommunion.org/commission/content/members.cfm

14. "submissions of evidence":
    www.anglicancommunion.org/acns/articles/37/00/acns3713.cfm

15. "The story told":
     Thanks to Simon Sarmiento and Professor Diarmaid N. J. MacCulloch for comment.

16. "Since the 1978 Lambeth Conference":
     www.anglicancommunion.org/commission/documents/ commissioning.pdf

17. Rite of Commissioning:
     www.anglicancommunion.org/commission/documents/ 20040209commissioning.pdf

     A Charge from Archbishop Rowan Williams:
     www.anglicancommunion.org/commission/documents/200402charge.pdf

18. "the commission reported itself saddened":
     www.anglicancommunion.org/commission/news/ windsor1communique.cfm

19. "In April, Archbishop Eames":
     www.anglicancommunion.org/commission/documents/200404eames.cfm

20. "Archbishop Drexel Gomez":
     www.anglicancommunion.org/acns/articles/38/00/acns3828.cfm

21. "laconic press release":
     www.anglicancommunion.org/acns/articles/38/00/acns3846.cfm

22. "private document":
     www.episcopalchurch.org/3577_26104_ENG_HTM.htm

23. "Résumé of submissions by individuals to the Lambeth Commission on Communion up to June 12th":
     www.anglicancommunion.org/commission/documents/ 200406overview.pdf

24. "Notes on the submissions to the Lambeth Commission on Communion":
     www.anglicancommunion.org/commission/documents/ResumeSep04.cfm

25. Foreword:
     www.anglicancommunion.org/windsor2004/index.cfm

26. All citations from The Windsor Report:
     www.anglicancommunion.org/windsor2004/downloads/ windsor2004full.pdf

27. A recollection of that little-known history is useful in understanding the context to which the commission refers. Florence Li Tim-Oi reportedly first experienced a call to ordained ministry in 1931 and was made a deacon of the Diocese of Hong Kong and South China in 1941. She was given charge of the Anglican congregation in neutral Macao. When a priest could no longer travel from Japanese-occupied Hong Kong to preside at the congregation's Eucharists, as a wartime measure Assistant Bishop Mok Sau Tseng

licensed Tim-Oi to do so as a deacon. In June 1943, Bishop Ronald Owen Hall wrote to Archbishop of Canterbury William Temple:

> If I could reach her physically I should ordain her priest rather than give her permission as that seems to me more contrary to the tradition and meaning of the ordained ministry than to ordain a woman.... I'm not an advocate for the ordination of women. I am, however, determined that no prejudices should prevent the congregations committed to my care having the sacraments of the Church.

In fact, Hall may have had other feelings about the issue. At a celebration of Tim-Oi's diamond ordination anniversary, Hall's son Christopher, also a priest, recalled, "What mattered to my father... was that God had already given to you the gift of priesthood, which for three years you had been licensed to exercise, and your ministry had been manifestly blessed. Who was he to deny what God had already done?"

On January 25, 1944, Hall ordained Tim-Oi as a priest in Hsinxing, Guandong, China. Again he wrote to Temple that he had done so not on account of "the theoretical view of the equality of men and women but the needs of my people for the sacraments." By that time Temple had already written back to Hall, stating that "you may still be acting under the dictation of the emergency but you would be doing something of which the effects would be permanent and could not be terminated."

When Hall's letter arrived telling him of the ordination, Temple replied that, although the theological arguments for not ordaining women "seem quite desperately futile... I cannot think that in any circumstances whatever an individual Bishop has the right to take such a step which is most certainly contrary to all the laws and precedents of the Church... and I therefore feel obliged to tell you that I do profoundly deplore the action that you took and have to regard it as *ultra vires* [beyond your powers]" (Source: *www.womenpriests.org/related/rose_08.asp*). Because of wartime restrictions, news of Tim-Oi's ordination was slow to reach the rest of the world. When it did, although Hong Kong's Diocesan Synod unanimously supported Hall's action, it caused much agitation in the Church of England. Though initially entered into the Church Missionary Society's Native Clergy Register, Tim-Oi's name was removed in June 1944. (Source: *www.fulcrum-anglican.org.uk/docs/2004/12/20041206michaelpoon.pdf*: *Maintaining the Bonds of Affection and the Discovering of Objects of Love: An East Asian Response to the Windsor Report 2004*, Michael Nai-Chiu Poon, Singapore.) An editorial in the *Church Times* of July 1944 opined that Hall "neither considered the wider implications of his action, nor consulted wiser heads than his own. He preferred to play a lone hand, not like a civilized leader who is himself subject to constitutional authority, but like a wild man of the woods...."

After the war, the Chinese bishops censured Hall, and told Tim-Oi that either she must resign her orders or Hall must resign as bishop. Tim-Oi surrendered her license to officiate, but insisted she never resigned her orders as a priest.

The 1948 Lambeth Conference rejected a proposal from the Chung Hua Sheng Kung Hui (Holy Catholic Church in China) that would allow a deaconess to be ordained to the priesthood for an experimental period of twenty years. The bishops declared that "such an experiment would be against the tradition and order and would gravely affect the internal and external relations of the Anglican Communion.... The time has not come for its further formal consideration" (Source: *www.anglicancommunion.org/acns/archive/ 1948/in1948.htm*).

Meanwhile, Tim-Oi served as rector of a church in Hepu, China, until it was closed in 1951 (the Diocese of Hong Kong represented the main body of the Anglican Church in China after Mao Tse-Tung's government came to power in 1949, and churches in China were not reopened until 1979). In 1981, Tim-Oi, by then in her seventies, went to live with relatives in Canada. She served as a priest in parishes in Montreal and Toronto and was a special guest at the 1988 Lambeth Conference.

28. Some commentators have taken issue with this characterization of the process, noting that, at the time, the Anglican Consultative Council was criticized for having exceeded its limitations as a consultative and not a legislative body.

29. Ironically, as observer Simon Sarmiento of the Anglicans Online Web site pointed out at the time, the official stance immediately following passage of the resolution seemed to be that it would not have much practical effect on the life of the Communion.

> The debate was noticeable for the absence of American speakers. The only ECUSA bishops who spoke were the Bishop of Maryland, Robert Ihloff, and Suffragan Bishop of New York, Catherine Roskam, both of whom spoke against the amendment to clause (d) from the Archbishop of Tanzania. Bishop Roskam said that to adopt this amendment would be "evangelical suicide" in New York and San Francisco, leading to a pyrrhic victory and a divided church. Bishop Russell of Grahamstown, South Africa, was the only other bishop that spoke against the amendment although twice as many people opposed the amendment as voted against or abstained on the overall motion.... The unsolved mystery of yesterday is why 100 or so bishops [out of a total of 740] attending the Conference apparently did not vote at all. (Source: *http://justus.anglican.org/newsarchive/ lambeth98/sjn15.html.*)

In a speech to the Anglican Church League in October 1998, conservative Bishop Paul Barnett of North Sydney characterized the subsection on sexuality as strongly liberal, but said its resolution was "pointedly and cleverly amended by a number of African bishops" in a plenary session chaired by Archbishop Eames. The amended resolution "passed with a 7 to 1 landslide majority." Barnett partially attributed the conservative victory to "the infrastructure provided by the conservative Americans" at a nearby Franciscan chaplaincy on the University of Kent campus. "A war room was set up in the Franciscan Centre with computers, faxes and mobile phones.... On the eve of the Plenary a large meeting was held in which we persuaded the Africans to drop their rather extreme resolutions and to amend the resolution of the sub-section" (Source: *www.rci.rutgers.edu/lcrew/lambeth98/lambeth121.html*).

By contrast, in a sermon during the evening worship of August 7, just two days after the vote, Archbishop Khotso Makhulu of the Church of the Province of Central Africa warned:

> The tenor of some of our discussions can only be described as "frenzied." The tone in which they were expressed was devoid of the love of God. We have had tyrants using the Bible as armor, and words spoken from this very spot that were aimed to wound and to score debating points.... There were those in this conference who have power, those who want it and want it badly, those who want to use it — whether by being utterly articulate or experts at procedural devices — those who have the "lollie" [money] and know exactly how to use it to best advantage. Sadly, we have equally had those who have been marginalized in our midst — some are confused and others remain wounded. From my background, I want to say here and now, I have resisted tyranny all my life and nor will I ever tolerate it from those who claim the love of the Bible over everyone else. Let not the intolerance of a variety of contexts inexorably lead us to intolerance, which, if unchecked, will find us with a band of vigilantes and fundamentalists. (Source: *www.rci.rutgers.edu/ lcrew/lambeth98/lambeth67.html*)

30. Statement:
    www.anglicancommunion.org/acns/articles/38/75/acns3897.cfm

31. Statement:
    www.anglicancommunion.org/acns/articles/38/75/acns3893.cfm

32. Statement:
    www.anglicancommunion.org/acns/articles/39/00/acns3901.cfm

33. Statement:
    www.anglicancommunion.org/acns/articles/38/75/acns3894.cfm

34. Statement:
    www.anglicancommunion.org/acns/articles/38/75/acns3899.cfm

35. Statement:
    www.anglicancommunion.org/acns/articles/38/75/acns3898.cfm

36. Statement:
    www.anglicancommunion.org/acns/articles/39/00/acns3902.cfm

37. Statement:
www.anglicancommunion.org/commission/responses/southerncone.cfm

38. Statement:
www.anglicancommunion.org/commission/responses/aotearoa.cfm

39. Statement:
www.anglicancommunion.org/acns/articles/39/00/acns3903.cfm

40. "Reception Reference Group":
www.anglicancommunion.org/commission/reception/index.cfm

41. Cameron:
*www.anglicancommunion.org/commission/reception/docs/
Bruce%20Cameron%20Report.pdf*

42. Analysis:
www.anglicancommunion.org/commission/reception/docs/analysis.pdf

43. Communique:
www.anglicancommunion.org/acns/articles/39/00/acns3948.cfm

44. "Official reports":
www.episcopalchurch.org/3577_59160_ENG_HTM.htm

45. "Unofficial reports":
*http://churchnewspaper.com/englandonsunday/index.php?read=
on&number_key=5758&title=Behind%20the%20scenes%20at%20the
%20Primates'%20Meeting,%20part%201*

*http://churchnewspaper.com/englandonsunday/index.php?read=
on&number_key=5758&title=Behind%20the%20scenes%20at%20the
%20Primates'%20Meeting,%20part%202*

46. "Archbishop Gregory Venables":
*http://churchtimes.co.uk/80256FA1003E05C1/httpPublicPages/
6622FD58E830934380256FC00044D518?opendocument*

47. Stephen Bates:
www.guardian.co.uk/uk_news/story/0,3604,1430275,00.html

48. *www.churchtimes.co.uk/80256FA1003E05C1/httpPublicPages/
6622FD58E830934380256FC00044D518?opendocument*

49. Coda:
*www.anglicancommunion.org/commission/documents/
RWilliamsMoralDecisions.cfm*

Thanks for review and comment are due to Matthew Davies of Episcopal News Service; the Rev. Tobias S. Haller, BSG; Professor Diarmaid N. J. MacCulloch, DD, FBA, Oxford University; and Simon Sarmiento, UK-Europe editor of Anglicans Online (*http://anglicansonline.org/*) and Thinking Anglicans (*http://thinkinganglicans.org.uk/*).